THE ULTIMATE GUIDE TO
TO
SMALL GAME AND
VARMINT HUNTING

Books by H. Lea Lawrence

Prowling Papa's Waters (1992)

The Archer's and Bowhunter's Bible (1992)

The Small Game and Varmint Hunter's Bible (1994)

The Outdoor Photographer's Bible (with Aubrey Watson) (1997)

The Fly Fisherman's Guide to the Great Smoky Mountains National Park (1998)

A Hemingway Odyssey: Special Places in His Life (1999)

THE ULTIMATE GUIDE TO SMALL GAME AND VARMINT HUNTING

How to Hunt Squirrels, Rabbits, Woodchucks, Coyotes, Foxes, and Other Game Animals

H. LEA LAWRENCE

The Lyons Press
Guilford, Connecticut
An imprint of The Globe Pequot Press

This book is dedicated to my sons, David and Charles, who are special individuals and excellent outdoorsmen.

Copyright © 2002 by H. Lea Lawrence
All photographs copyright © the author unless otherwise noted.

The Lyons Press is an imprint of The Globe Pequot Press.

Printed in the United States of America

10 9 8 7 6 5 4 3

ISBN 978-1-58574-566-1

Library of Congress Cataloging-in-Publication Data is available on file

Lawrence, H. Lea, 1930-
    The ultimate guide to small game and varmint hunting : how to hunt squirrels, rabbits, hares, woodchucks, coyotes, foxes, and more / H. Lea Lawrence.
        p. cm.
Includes bibliographical references and index.
    ISBN 1-58574-566-9 (alk. paper)
    1. Small game hunting. 2. Varmint hunting. I. Title.
    SK340 .L38 2002
    799.2'5—dc21

2002003569

ACKNOWLEDGMENTS

I wish to acknowledge the invaluable assistance of Rick Masters in regard to both technical and general matters; to Aubrey Watson, an astute professional whose personal interest in the project helped him create an array of photographs of exceptional quality; to the state and federal agencies for the loan of photographs; and to the many friends and contacts in the shooting and hunting industry who supplied materials and illustrations vital to the creation of this book.

CONTENTS

Contents

PHOTO CREDITS

*Neal & MJ Mishler 5, 28, 34, 60, 116, 132, 157, 180
Aubrey Watson 14, 17, 21, 23, 24, 44, 51, 52, 53, 54, 55, 67, 71, 72, 74, 76, 78, 80–87, 93, 97, 98, 101–104, 109, 110, 111 (top), 112, 117, 119, 121, 125, 128, 142–146, 148, 151, 154, 162, 163, 164, 175, 177, 184, 186, 188–191, 200, 202, 203, 206, 207, 210, 218, 219, 221, 227, 228
Jay Cassell 168
Joel Arrington 105
U.S. Fish and Wildlife Service 4, 31, 56, 57, 59, 170
Thompson Center 19, 45
Mossy Oak 20*

FOREWORD

by Peter J. Fiduccia

The morning sun was just about to peak over the horizon when we finally settled into our setup. It was very cold and I welcomed the sunshine, hoping it would help warm me up. In front of us was a huge field surrounded by thick woods and swamps. The pungent aroma of soil and cut timothy grass filled my nostrils. I liked the smell. Between the cold and the aromas, I felt alive. I guess that's part of any hunt—the aromas of the outdoors, I mean. Thirty yards away, I could see the electronic decoy rabbit Gordy had placed in the field to help entice even the most cautious of coyotes to come in. A gentle but frigid morning breeze pushed lightly at my face. Gordy asked softly, "Ready?" "Yes," I whispered. I was here as a cameraman to tape a segment of a coyote hunting video Gordy was producing. I had never hunted predators before.

Gordy said, "Here goes. Stay still and keep your eyes peeled." I flipped the camo rag over myself and the camera and placed the lens through the small hole in the rag. Gordy blew several excited rabbit sounds. Within seconds, a coyote yipped with excitement. Gordy called again and this time the coyote didn't respond. I wondered why. Moments later I understood. He didn't have to. There he was, about seventy-five yards from us, making a beeline straight for the electronic rabbit that was pulsating and withering like it was about to keel over dead at any moment.

I began to roll tape as soon as I picked up the dog in the lens. The next thing I knew the coyote had covered about 150 yards and was in shooting range. But then something went wrong. As the coyote got close enough for Gordy to shoot, it instantly whirled in full stride and headed off in a different direction at warp 9.9!

Before I could ask, Gordy said, "Smart aren't they? He spotted or smelled something he didn't like—maybe the glare from the lens of the camera. Who knows—that's predator hunting. We'll have to move to another setup now." Only then did I begin to understand the type of cunning animal we were dealing with. Over the next two days, Gordy called in several more coyotes and we did take a few. But there were just as many that either winded or spotted us, or were just too cautious to be fooled by the calls and decoy. In any event, that was it. I was hooked on hunting coyotes.

It's been several years since then, and now I regularly plan to hunt all types of predators throughout the season. Predator hunting is one of the most challenging and exciting sports around. It takes skill and determination to call predators consistently. It also takes conditioning. Many hunters, both in the East and West, endure all types of weather conditions when pursuing coyotes and other predators. They understand that part of the hunt also means having the stamina to hike for miles either in the freezing cold or under the blazing sun in order to outwit one of nature's most worthy and cunning adversaries: the predator. To match wits with those who hunt to survive is the ultimate test in one's own true hunting skills. The outstanding section on predator hunting in this book will not only help you to become a better predator hunter, but it will also instill in you the obsession with the sport as well!

When I was just starting out as a hunter, most of my days afield were spent hunting small game. Unlike big-game hunting, small-game hunting does not require a lot of detailed planning or extended trips away from home. The small-game hunter, unlike the waterfowler or big-game hunter, doesn't have to stay out in rain, snow, or freezing conditions to bag game, and he doesn't have to seek his quarry far from home either. In fact, small-game hunting doesn't really require anything more than a desire to venture out for a day's hike into the woods and fields close to home.

America is blessed with an abundance of small-game animals and birds of assorted types, and all at healthy population levels throughout the country. The habitats of these different species frequently overlap each other, so hunters chasing after one type of animal often find other types of small game to challenge them as well. In addition, most state game departments do a fine job managing the nation's small-game populations. In turn, we are provided with plenty of hunting opportunities for our fellow outdoorsmen and women.

But small-game hunting is more than just the taking of a fast-running rabbit or hare, or trying to outwit a wily woodchuck, or pursuing the frustrating and quick-thinking squirrel. No, it's much more than that for those who take up the sport. Being able to walk through an autumn forest with all the colors of the leaves assaulting one's senses, breathing and smelling the air, and observing other wildlife and the surroundings are the true rewards. Taking small game is just the added bonus. Whether you're hunting for hours alone or with a companion, these elements are yours to enjoy during a small-game hunt afield. It helps both the seasoned veteran and the novice gain a balance with nature that brings an equilibrium to all those who hunt.

There is no other type of hunting that helps introduce first-time hunters to the sport better than small-game hunting. It alone has been the inspiration for millions of sportsmen to join the fraternity of hunters.

So sit back and page through this book and be whisked off to some fall woodlot where the sounds of beagles harmonizing as they gain on their cottontail quarry fills the air. Or, where the alarm cries of a squirrel darting around the backside of a tree to avoid your getting a bead on him ring deeply in your ears. Or, where at the last moment, just before you flip your rifle's safety off, the woodchuck you had in the crosshairs disappears back into his hole. This is the excitement of small-game hunting. After reading this book, you'll be motivated to clean your shotgun—even though it's probably already clean. Or maybe just reorganize your small-game gear. In other words, this book will get the adrenaline flowing in your veins—and before you realize it, another small-game hunting season will be underway!

INTRODUCTION

SMALL GAME

AND VARMINTS: WHICH IS WHICH?

It isn't possible to clearly separate the terms small game and varmint, because there are instances where certain species may occupy either category according to how they're viewed by hunters and/or game agencies. Many examples exist, so rules governing how these animals are classified vary from location to location. Also, a maze of regulations governs the manner in which they may be taken and at what times of the year they may be pursued.

Because of the volume and complexity of these myriad differences in the regulations, it would be impossible, or at least impractical, to attempt to list them. In addition, there are periodic changes in the status of certain birds and animals, so the information couldn't be fully relied upon from year to year. The best solution is for the individual to check out the laws applying to the place where he plans to hunt.

Almost as diversified as the elements just noted is the overall variety of weapons involved. Farm boys often begin hunting with slingshots, which could be considered the low end of the spectrum, while the super-accurate, highly sophisticated, long-range varmint rifles represent the high end. In between is a kaleidoscopic assortment of both modern and primitive rifles, pistols, and shotguns, as well as archery equipment. Small game and varmints are "everyman" sports.

SMALL GAME

The tradition of small game hunting in civilized America dates back to 1620 when the first Pilgrims stepped ashore at Plymouth Rock. Having accomplished their goal of reaching a sanctuary in the New World, the matter of providing food and shelter for the colony was of principal importance. Resources for both needs were present. Raw materials for the construction of buildings—wood, stone, sand and clay—were plentiful in the region, and there was an abundance of game in the fields and forests.

For two particular reasons, small game became the main source of the meat consumed by the inhabitants of Plymouth. First, it was readily available in great quantities, and second, it was what could be most easily harvested with the somewhat primitive weapons they possessed. Their blunderbusses—muskets with flaring muzzles—were designed to throw charges of pellets just as modern shotguns do. The difference was that there was no constriction in the barrels to concentrate the charge, so they could truly be called "scatterguns." More than 200 years would pass before a choke system was devised.

Despite this handicap, the guns had a range of up to 40 yards, and they were quite adequate for all kinds of small game. The rifles of that period, on the other hand, were mostly matchlocks of poor quality, because the monarchy from which the settlers had fled didn't want efficient firearms in the hands of the general public. The performance of their rifles left much to be desired, and it wasn't until after 1700 that there was much improvement. That was when the first German settlers arrived and began to manufacture the truly fine and accurate Pennsylvania long rifles that were to gain lasting fame. These muzzleloaders set a new standard for all blackpowder guns that were to follow.

The greatest advantage of the Pennsylvania rifles was that they could be produced in a variety of calibers built specifically for an intended purpose. The guns of the earlier years were mostly big bore weapons designed mainly for killing people. They were cumbersome and virtually useless for all but large animals. Tales of early hunters "barking" squirrels—stunning them by hitting the limb on which they were sitting—are true, but it wasn't to demonstrate their marksmanship. They did it because the big bullets would blow a squirrel to pieces. Once the squirrels were knocked out of the tree and on the ground, they could be fully dispatched.

The light, graceful Pennsylvania rifles with smaller bores were much better suited for squirrels, rabbits, and similar kinds of game. They were remarkably accurate, and they quickly became the favorites of hunters. It was a point of pride to be a skillful marksman, and shooting matches were a popular form of entertainment among the frontiersmen.

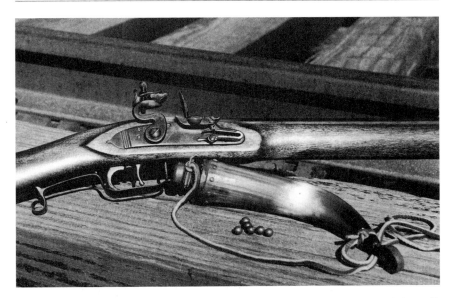

The Pennsylvania long rifle was a great improvement over the blunderbusses of the earliest settlers. A muzzleloader with a flintlock action, it was the first reliable and accurate gun on the American frontier.

As more settlers arrived from England and Europe and the westward movement continued, small game remained an important part of the pioneers' diet while on the move. Hunters were assigned to forage for game as they traveled along. Even when their goals were reached and homesteads created, small game continued to be the most important source of meat. Cows were for milk, poultry primarily for eggs and down, sheep for wool and often swine were sold or bartered rather than slaughtered for home use. Besides, in most areas the amount of small game seemed limitless and easy to harvest, sort of like manna from heaven.

Meanwhile, in the East, civilization was firmly taking hold as more families put down permanent roots. The population was mostly rural, and farms were producing ever-increasing amounts of food. Still, though small game was no longer essential for survival, it remained a substantial and desirable supplement to most farm families' diet.

In many cases, the responsibility for collecting squirrels and rabbits was delegated to youngsters. This was hardly an unpleasant assignment, being fun rather than a chore. Most young hunters cut their teeth on small game, and this was the basis for a tradition that remains dominant. Small game hunting continues to be the most popular of all of the shooting sports.

The initial notion that there would always be an unending supply of game eventually proved to be badly in error as dramatic changes began to occur. Human populations increased and more pressure was brought to bear on most wildlife populations. Numbers declined, and although evidence of this was obvious by the late 1800s, it was after the turn of the century before the alarm was sounded loudly enough to end unregulated hunting. Seasons and bag limits were set, and license fees were imposed as a means of supporting wildlife agencies and their programs.

While the numbers of most big game species were reduced to low levels (and sometimes completely eliminated in some locations), small game was affected less seriously. Agricultural practices provided ample food and cover for rabbits and other forms of ground-dwelling wildlife, and there was a wealth of woodlots and forested areas that supported good squirrel populations. Under such conditions, both reproduction and survival rates were high. The farm boy with a single shot .22 rifle or shotgun over his shoulder could be assured of plenty of action.

Hunting was a way of life in the rural communities, and shooting was a well-accepted form of sport and recreation. Many small towns had shooting fraternities or lodges that sponsored regular shooting matches among their own members or those from other lodges. These were highly popular hometown affairs that drew crowds of spectators.

Also, some of the arms and ammunition manufacturers hired professional shooters who traveled around the country staging exhibitions. The public regarded these individuals as celebrities, and an appearance by one of these experts was usually accompanied by numerous receptions and social events. The husband/wife team of Ad and Plinky Topperwein was probably the best known, but there were many others who toured the nation to great acclaim.

Of course, the most noted of the professional shooters was Annie Oakley, who gained fame as a member of Buffalo Bill's Wild West Show. When she arrived on the scene, Buffalo Bill's "top gun" was Frank Butler. Annie was a better shot and quickly became the star attraction. In the meantime, however, she and Frank fell in love and were married, so this, too, became another his-and-hers shooting team.

Despite changes in agricultural and other land use practices, greatly increased hunting pressure and more limited access to private property, in most areas there's still an abundance of small game and plenty of places to hunt. Across the nation are millions of acres open to the public on the many national and state forests, federal and state wildlife management areas and public hunting lands. In recent years there has also been a tremendous amount of prime hunting land made available to the public on many of the huge tracts owned by private timber companies. This has significantly increased opportunity, particularly in the eastern part of the nation where the principal amount of small game hunting occurs.

Small game hunting continues to be the most popular of all of the shooting sports, and the outlook for the foreseeable future is bright. Neither of the two most-sought species requires special kinds of management. Squirrels fare quite well as long as they have access to hardwood stands, and rabbits are prolific in places where agricultural practices provide food and cover.

However, something else is necessary for the perpetuation of this type of hunting. There is a great need to encourage and reestablish the wonderful father/son, or father/daughter bonds that help pass the hunting tradition from generation to generation. Hunting is a special kind of experience that has many physical, mental and aesthetic benefits that last a lifetime and contribute to an individual's character.

One other thing: There are strong anti-hunting and anti-gun forces that would like to deny Americans the opportunity to enjoy this traditional and treasured form of outdoor recreation. Their arguments are based on emotion rather than intelligent thinking, and are directly opposed to the freedom of choice that is our heritage. Still, they pose a threat that must be taken seriously by every hunter.

VARMINTS

Varmints offer the hunter extra shooting opportunity of an exciting sort, both during and in between the regular seasons. Traditionally, varmints have been regarded as incidental to mainstream hunting except for a relatively small following of dedicated shooters. However, in recent years this has changed. Varminting has become very popular, and there are many hunters who find it the most challenging and satisfying of all pursuits available in the field.

The sport offers special advantages, one of which is that many of the creatures included in this category are unprotected. They can be sought anytime of the year. Another is that competition for these species is markedly less than for game birds and animals.

Also, because there are so many different kinds of varmints throughout North America, there's opportunity almost everywhere.

Varmints have a long history in this country. While small game was indeed a blessing for the early settlers, it didn't take long for them to discover wildlife species that were detrimental to their daily lives in one way or another. Along with the good came the bad.

The problems became apparent once the colonists prepared ground for the first planting. From the time fields were sown right on through harvest time, crops were plagued by various kinds of marauders. As soon as seeds were placed in the ground, crows and other birds plucked them out. When the first sprouts pushed up through the earth, woodchucks began feasting on the bounty. And throughout the entire growing season, farmers fought a constant battle with vandals of one kind or another.

Yet crops weren't the only targets. Domestic fowl were always in danger from foxes, weasels, bobcats and hawks. The young of some domestic livestock also fell victim to the larger predators.

The best defense — or offense — against these damaging creatures was the gun, so just as the tradition of hunting small game began at the Plymouth Colony, so did the tradition of varmint hunting.

At the outset it wasn't viewed as a sport. Rather, it was an almost everyday task necessary for the protection of crops, livestock and, in some instances, human beings. The goal was to eradicate the offenders, or at least to eliminate as many as possible.

The predatory species involved were called by lots of names. In the language of the colonists, the terms vermin, pirates, brigands, ravishers, thieves and looters were all used, and no doubt some profane ones, as well! Some of these may still be in use, but today varmint is the word most commonly used to describe the "bad guys."

Webster defines varmint as "an animal or bird considered as a pest," and "an animal classed as vermin and unprotected by game law." This is a definition that can be broadly interpreted, and in the case of our forefathers, it was. As the westward movement progressed, it was applied to anything that posed a threat or annoyance of any kind. Reptiles, hawks, owls and eagles, rodents, grizzly bears, mountain lions, and wild horses were included. Even certain people earned the epithet.

Today it's much more limited in scope, and varmint is now generally used in reference to smaller creatures. Yet there's no universal agreement across the country as to what is placed in this category. The reasons for this disparity are soundly based, many of which relate to range, distribution and population levels. Others refer to economic or agricultural impact, and some of these are based on competition with more desirable species. This can occur in adjoining states or provinces where the only difference is a boundary line and the opinions of personnel within the individual wildlife agencies. Unfortunately, trained game managers don't always have the final say. Some destructive and undesirable animals end up on the protected list because of efforts by animal activists, anti-hunters, and other elements often driven by emotion rather than by scientific facts.

There have been other changes in the varmint picture. Over the years some predators that once economically impacted crops and livestock have been reduced in numbers to the point where they no longer remain significant threats. In some instances wildlife agencies manage these varmints only to whatever degree is necessary to achieve a reasonable balance and avoid overkill. Other species once branded as detrimental, such as hawks, owls, and eagles, have been placed on the protected list almost everywhere. Even some of the reptiles now fall into the protected category, and in some cases even poisonous species can't be killed. Snapping turtles still offer opportunity in most places, and plinking them with a .22 can be a great asset to a lake or pond where waterfowl or shorebirds nest, since these creatures are effective predators. They devour young birds, and are able to maim or cripple adults.

Even with such exceptions, there's no shortage of varmints that can be sought. Throughout the continent all kinds of opportunities exist, and at some locations, a veritable potpourri of choices is offered. Alaska is a good example, where bats, shrews, rats, mice, porcupines, raccoons, lynx, starlings, cormorants, crows, foxes, and coyotes can be hunted in all or some of the 26 units, some with no season or bag limits. Too, in most places virtually all of the rodents are unprotected, as are a few birds, although crows are the only ones that get serious attention.

There have been changes in the ways in which animals and birds, game or varmints, can be taken. Once, any type of motorized vehicles, including boats, was legal, as were airplanes and helicopters. There are now various federal and state laws that strictly govern all of these things. One, The Airborne Hunting Act of 1956 (and subsequent amendments in 1971 and 1972) effectively closed the door on the use of any type of aircraft for hunting or harassing any fish, birds, or animals. The only exceptions are in cases where predation permits are issued to landowners suffering damage or are used by authorized federal or state game and fish agencies. As for game birds and animals other than migratory waterfowl, there are many places where vehicles can be used, but in each case there are specific rules that apply regarding the hows, wheres and whens.

Yet even though restrictions have been placed on many birds and animals with good reason, those that have been the main interest of varmint hunters over the years—woodchucks, prairie dogs, crows, coyotes, bobcats, and others—have been little affected. They're still highly prolific; and farmers, ranchers and landowners want them eliminated or reduced in numbers. Because of this desire, varmint shooters often gain access to places denied other hunters. Since most wildlife agencies agree that this is the best way to control or manage a varmint population, everybody's happy. Looking ahead, there are good reasons to believe that this sport is going to remain high profile and will supplement the losses in opportunity that occur in other areas of hunting.

One reason is that interest in varmint shooting is constantly growing. Many hunters who once considered it simply a pastime to fill gaps between regular seasons have become full-time participants. Pressure on many game species has increased, resulting in shorter seasons and leaner bag limits. As this occurs, shooters eager for more action and additional time in the field are attracted to this year-around opportunity.

Something else: once hunters become aware of the challenges and special skills involved, varmint shooting quickly gains stature. And it isn't unusual for it to gain priority over some once-favorite pursuits.

Finally, there's one varmint which has managed to establish itself over the entire continent, and which will perpetually be around to match wits with varminters. Sly, cunning and unpredictable, it stands as the ultimate challenge.

Stay tuned!

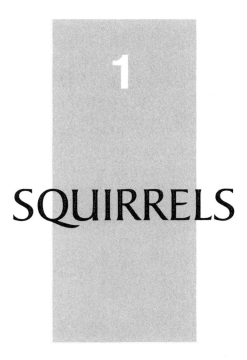

SQUIRRELS

Sometimes scientific, or taxonomic, names are poetic, and sometimes they are specific. However, in the instance of Sciuridae, the squirrel family, neither seems to apply. In Latin, this means "shade-tail," referring to the habit some of the species exhibit in holding a bushy tail over their backs. That's hardly inspiring, and it also isn't accurate, since most of the animals in this category have short, slim tails that would produce a very little shade, if at all.

In a way, this isn't surprising, especially when the broad diversity of the squirrel family is considered. It encompasses: 63 species; sizes that range from the tiny chipmunks that weigh less than 2 ounces to the large hoary marmots that may attain 20 pounds; distribution from Mexico to the Arctic; members classed as game, nongame, varmints, protected or endangered; and burrowers, tree-dwellers, and even some that "fly."

Small game hunters, though, aren't bothered by this seeming complexity. For example, of the more than five-dozen species, only three that are classified as tree squirrels are of major importance to small game hunters. It's a

There is no better way for a youngster to learn squirrel hunting than with a father or other experienced adult.

much different situation where varmint hunters are concerned, but that will be discussed later.

Of this trio of true "shade-tails," the one most familiar to hunters, as well as the general public, is the Gray Squirrel. This highly popular game animal is generally present wherever nut trees are found, whether in large hardwood stands or small woodlots. It's also equally at home in urban settings, and few city parks and suburban neighborhoods within their extensive range are without the gray squirrel.

Squirrels and nuts are synonymous. Acorns are the most abundant mast crop throughout their range, but squirrels also feed on hickory nuts, walnuts, pecans, and beechnuts. They bury nuts, but despite common belief, they don't recall the locations. However, they are able to smell them, even through snow cover, so they retrieve many at times when food is most vital. Yet while mast is a mainstay during the fall and winter months, their overall menu includes many other items. Squirrels eat maple, tulip and pine tree seeds, fruit, mushrooms, and other fungi, as well as flowers and young buds. In agricultural areas, they often ravage cornfields from the time the ears first appear until harvest time.

In some locations hunters refer to grays as cat squirrels, probably because of the mewing sounds they sometimes make. Another possible reason is their quick, darting "catlike" movements.

Gray squirrels occupy cavities in trees in the winter, usually natural openings caused by disease or fire, or holes made by woodpeckers. These dens are lined with leaves and provide snug quarters during harsh weather. In extreme conditions, squirrels may remain in their dens for up to several days, but unlike some other rodents they don't hibernate, staying active throughout the winter. In the summer they build leaf nests that are perched in crotches or in forks of limbs. Some of these are ball-shaped and well constructed, with living space inside; others are flimsy, flat structures used mainly as platforms for sunning or loafing.

The major feeding activity takes place in early morning and late afternoon, yet sometimes all day if food is scarce. Though seldom observed, on moonlit nights in the springtime, they often feed on tender tree buds. In times of overpopulation or mast failures, mass migrations may occur as a survival attempt.

Although this species is usually quite uniform in color, with gray above and white underparts, there is a black phase common to parts of its northern

Gray Squirrel

range. There are also scattered colonies of albino gray squirrels, most of which are found in towns or cities where they are protected. Adults weigh from 14 to 25 ounces.

Of all the tree squirrels, gray squirrels have the largest range. They're found in all of the eastern U.S., southern Manitoba, Iowa, and the eastern parts of North Dakota, Oklahoma, Kansas and Texas.

The Fox Squirrel is a larger, less graceful animal than the gray, and throughout its range there are several distinct color phases. In the North the pattern is yellowish-brown on the upper parts, and yellow to orange underparts; in the South they are grayish-grizzled above, whitish below, and have a dark head and white nose. Other variations are: specimens that are all black except for white-tipped nose and ear, and others that are steel blue. Weights vary according to locations, and usually average about two pounds in adults. However, specimens of over three pounds do occur.

This species occupies a broad spectrum of habitat types: oak-hickory hardwood stands, cypress and mangrove swamps, live oaks and mixed forests, and piney woods. They also are more inclined to open areas, inhabiting slim stands of trees along streams and rivers, thickets and urban areas.

Fox Squirrel

Fox squirrels have an appetite for almost anything they can find. All kinds of nuts, berries, seeds, bulbs, fruit, roots, insects, bird eggs, fungi, buds, and the inner bark of maple trees are relished. Like their cousins, they also will wreak havoc on cornfields. When foraging, they ordinarily travel considerable distances from their dens, usually moving along on the ground rather than through the trees. Also, seeing one in an open field isn't uncommon.

This species also occupies leaf nests in the summer, but these are nearly always nestled in the crotches of trees instead on upper or outer limbs. Because of their larger body size and weight, the latter often being twice that of a gray, they need such perches for greater stability. When resting or loafing, they stretch out on broad limbs and use their tail as a parasol, living up to their family name. In the winter, holes or cavities that afford plenty of space are preferred, since several animals may share dens during this period. In places where both fox and gray squirrels are present, there's little contact between the species, although it's likely they compete for den space when winter approaches.

Fox squirrels are early risers, popping out of their nests or dens at first light and bounding out through the woods to dine on whatever they can find. With the need for a greater amount of food than gray squirrels, they go about this activity with zest, and usually for a longer period. Once satisfied, they either begin roaming or retire for an after-breakfast nap.

Extensive hardwood clearing in the Northeast has reduced fox squirrel numbers; and their presence has been eliminated in the New England states, most of New Jersey and parts of New York and Pennsylvania. Otherwise, they're found throughout the eastern U.S. and west to the Dakotas, northeastern Colorado and eastern Texas.

The Western Gray Squirrel bears a close resemblance to its eastern relatives except that it has numerous white-tipped hairs on the upper parts that give it a more silvery appearance, and the back of the ears are reddish-brown. The weight range is from 12 to 34 ounces.

These squirrels are found mainly in the redwood and hardwood forests common to the range they occupy. They build nests of shredded bark and leaves high above the ground for summer occupancy and spend the winter in tree hollows, cavities or woodpecker holes.

The habits are similar to the other two major tree squirrels. Chief foods are acorns, pine nuts, fungi, fruits, berries, bird eggs, and insects. This squirrel possesses a keen sense of smell and a superior memory that allows it to recover the majority of the nuts it buries.

This is the only squirrel in the West that's eagerly sought by hunters, and its range extends all the way from Washington to California. The areas of greatest abundance are the large forested areas in the coastal and inland mountain ranges.

Within the remaining tree-squirrel varieties, only one is hunted for food, while the rest are seldom, if ever, pursued for this purpose. One species is extremely low in numbers.

Abert's Squirrel is a brightly colored animal similar in size to the gray. It has dark gray upper parts accented with black and russet, and white underparts. Its trademark is its tufted ears. This species inhabits the Ponderosa forests and depends upon pine seeds and pinion nuts as its principal foods, but it also eats other items such as dropped antlers, fungi, berries, and weedy plants. It builds nests in tree crotches and lines them with shredded bark.

The range of the Abert's squirrel is in the isolated mountains of Arizona, Southeast Utah, Colorado, and New Mexico. A subspecies, the Kaibab Squirrel, is found only on the North Rim of the Grand Canyon and is considered endangered.

The Red Squirrel, sometimes called the pine squirrel or Chickaree, is small, with reddish to grayish back and side and whitish underparts. It occupies coniferous, hardwood, and mixed forests. Pine seeds are a major diet item, but it also will eat all of the other foods typical in tree squirrel menus. The range is broad, extending from the tree limit in the North and throughout most of Alaska and Canada; both the Rocky Mountain and Appalachian regions; the northeastern states; and Ohio, Indiana, Michigan, Illinois, Iowa, Minnesota, and Wisconsin.

Call the Douglas Squirrel a virtual twin of the red squirrel, since its nicknames are the same, as are its habits. One difference is that it's a very noisy animal with a wide variety of calls that are often an annoyance to hunters who are stalking other game. The range encompasses southwestern British Columbia, the western parts of Washington and Oregon, and western California.

The Southern Flying Squirrel has a silky fur that is grayish-brown above and white below, and large black eyes. Strictly nocturnal, these timid creatures occupy hardwood forests and prefer holes in trees as nests, although they sometimes build summer nests of leaves. Despite their ability to be airborne, they glide rather than fly. Berries, nuts, fungi, and insects are the main elements of their diet.

The range includes all of the eastern U.S. — except for New England and the lower portion of Florida — west to Minnesota and the eastern parts of Kansas and Texas.

The Northern Flying Squirrel is dark brown above and white below, and its habits are nearly identical to the southern variety. Its range is broader, however, extending all across Canada and into Alaska; in California, Idaho, Utah, Montana, and Wyoming; eastward through the northern states to New England; and into the Appalachians.

HUNTING METHODS

Lessons learned in squirrel hunting can be the most valuable training any hunter, young or old, can acquire. The things necessary for success include all of the elements required for seeking virtually any other small or big game species, which gave rise to the statement that "a good squirrel hunter can hunt anything."

Over the years millions of hunters have cut their teeth on squirrels. For a youngster, there's no better way to get started, especially if he or she is lucky enough to have a father or some other experienced person along as a teacher. It's impossible to forget the magic of the first squirrel hunt and the spine-tingling thrill of being in the woods in the spooky, pre-dawn atmosphere. It's a feeling that persists, no matter how many times the experience is repeated.

A youth looks over his first squirrel taken on a hunt with his father.

If one word could be seen as best associated with this sport, it would be stealth. Squirrels are very wary creatures, and they're definitely on their turf when being sought. This means that a hunter must be able to move through the woods silently, a procedure that once was called Indian-style. It isn't as easy as it might seem, since there are times when it is next to impossible to proceed noiselessly. Walking in dry leaves is the ultimate challenge, and those familiar with this situation know that it's as delicate an operation as balancing on a tightrope. The keys are patience and an ability to move very slowly and deliberately, picking out each spot where a foot is going to be placed with great caution. Stalking can be both the most difficult and most satisfying aspects of the sport, because succeeding means that you've outwitted one of the most sound-conscious creatures in the wild.

There's more to it than this one factor. Squirrels have eyesight quite as keen as their hearing, so quiet movement also means being as nearly invisible as possible. Also vital is that all movements be in slow motion. A quick turn of the head or a hand swatting away an insect is all it takes to bring a stalk to an instantaneous end, regardless of how well one has performed otherwise.

It must be remembered that these audio-visual capabilities aren't exclusive with the squirrels. It's a two-way street, and hunters can use them to their advantage just as effectively as the bushy-tails do. Squirrels make noises, too, and their movements often are far more flagrant than those of the hunter. The main thing is knowing what to look and listen for, and this takes experience. For instance, in the dim light of early morning, sounds are the only clues that can be relied upon. It's important to be able to distinguish the meaningful ones from those that are incidental.

One thing that definitely signals squirrel is the "whooshing" sound they make when leaping from tree to tree. When they're in motion, they aren't likely to detect other noises, so it's an ideal time to move and gain a little ground in the direction from which the sound comes. Often squirrels congregate on a particular feeding spot, which may be a single hickory or oak, and getting close and in position can result in a great beginning for the day!

Even if you can't get within range of the feeding location immediately, all you have to do is wait until the animals begin cutting nuts. This is another activity that muffles their ability to hear other sounds. The clatter of hulls and shells falling sounds like rain in the forest, and they make additional noises as

How close you approach your quarry depends on what kind of shooting equipment you're using. Smaller caliber rifles let you reach out a long way.

they dash back and forth gathering more nuts. The more squirrels that are in the tree, the greater the din becomes.

If there's sufficient light, spotting the early movement in the trees is easy, but there's a trick to visually covering a broad expanse of woods. The idea is to not focus on any particular spot. Instead, look straight ahead without any object in mind and let your eyes function like a wide-angle camera lens, taking advantage of your peripheral vision. This way you pick up every flicker of motion in a full 180-degree field of view.

How close you need to approach your quarry depends on what kind of shooting equipment you're using. A hunter with a .22 caliber rimfire rifle, particularly if scope-sighted, can pick off squirrels much farther away than a person using a shotgun. The latter has a maximum dependable killing range of less than 50 yards, while the rifle can be effective up to more than twice that distance. Usually, though, hunters prefer to get in as close as possible, partly so they can be more sure of their shots, but also because of the satisfaction in conducting a good stalk.

When woods are very dry, sitting is the most productive method. If you know the area, you'll be aware of where squirrels are feeding. Go to the spot

It's fairly easy to move up on squirrels when they're cutting nuts, because the noise they make obliterates other sounds.

before daylight and get yourself situated. Pick out a spot and clear the area of all leaves and twigs around where you plan to sit so any movement you make won't create noise. With this tactic, you're waiting for the squirrels to come to you instead of going to them.

One of the most enjoyable ways to hunt bushy-tails is floating down streams or rivers. This is a truly silent approach, and one that permits you to cover a lot of territory in a single morning or day. Some hunters using this tactic combine hunting squirrels with fishing, a form of the sport that is also very

The float tube provides an excellent way to hunt on smaller streams where boats aren't practical.

conducive to overnight trips. Drifting along quietly on a bright October day is exhilarating in itself, and when you can combine it with shooting squirrels, it's even better!

Canoes or flat-bottomed aluminum boats are ideal for this kind of hunting, which can be done either solo or with a partner. It's much more practical with two, since one person can handle the craft while the other keeps an eye out for action. The usual rule is one shot apiece between swapping roles.

Almost every state has waters that are suitable for this hunting technique, and topographical maps can help locate them. Picking stretches that pass through forested areas is best, but even those that have bordering strips of woods can be winners. Squirrels like to be close to water, and often they will occupy the trees that line the banks, particularly if those trees are mast-bearing. Too, stream and river bottomlands have plenty of the other foods squirrels eat throughout the year.

There's another kind of "bushytail boulevard" that's overlooked by most hunters, yet it's one that provides special advantages which can pay big dividends throughout the season. Also, it's an ace in the hole that can sometimes save the day when other approaches fail.

Canoes and flat-bottomed aluminum boats are ideal for float hunting for squirrels and provide a stable shooting platform.

What's the secret? Railroad tracks.

And the next question: why?

Think about it for a minute. Railroad tracks that pass through forested areas provide a way to penetrate the woods silently and with a minimum of effort. When drought conditions exist and the leaves are tinder dry, it's impossible to move quietly in the woods, regardless of how carefully you proceed. Walking along the tracks, however, allows you to be virtually silent. Then if squirrel activity is detected, you can proceed without having to attempt a lengthy and often futile stalk.

That's an example of an extreme situation, but using the rail-route is a very productive and enjoyable way to hunt no matter what conditions prevail. There are many benefits other than being able to stalk noiselessly. Another is that a lot of territory can be covered, increasing the odds for success. Sometimes tall trees along each side of the track overlap above it and create leafy bridges across which squirrels pass back and forth. This shooting opportunity, combined with the action hunters usually find directly adjacent to the tracks,

This tiny device which produces a red light that blinks continually for more than a month on one battery can be hung on a limb to assist a hunter in locating his stand before daylight.

can result in a limit of bushy-tails being bagged without ever stepping off the roadbed.

Locating woodlands through which railroads pass isn't difficult, and a look at a topographic map of your areas will probably disclose several that are worth investigating. And don't concentrate only on lines currently in use. There are many abandoned routes that may offer even better potential.

Recognizing the signs of squirrel activity enables hunters to have increased success. Scouting the woods and locating feeding sites in advance makes it possible to get in position before daylight on the morning of the hunt. According to the part of the country you're in and what kind of trees are found, identifying those to which squirrels are attracted at different times of the season is a big help. For instance, in the forests of the eastern U.S., beech may be the first mast, followed by white oak and hickory. Next will be the various other kinds of oak and black walnuts. At times when mast crops are meager, squirrels will cut pine cones, the fruit of Osage orange, and many seed-producing trees and shrubs which are normally low on the preference list. Don't forget that if there's a cornfield adjacent to or near the woods, this is also a prime spot to keep an eye on. Squirrels like corn at any stage of development, and in the fall when the crop is mature and ready for harvest, they usually pay daily visits to the fields. Generally, this activity takes place between midmorning and midafternoon, the times when they're most likely to be foraging on the ground.

Finding fresh cuttings of any of these items is a clue to where squirrels are active, so a foray into the woods ahead of the hunt can pay off well!

Though squirrels normally feed in early morning and late afternoon, as winter approaches they're liable to be foraging through the woods at any time of the day. Once the foliage is gone, most of this travel will be on the ground. In damp woods they're as silent as ghosts, and it takes a sharp eye to catch their movements.

Weather is an important factor. Squirrels are most active on calm days, whether sunny or cloudy. Windy days can be very "iffy," since they don't like conditions that prevent them from seeing and hearing things that may be threatening. Light rain usually isn't a deterrent, and it's great for a stalking hunter. During severe weather, squirrels will remain in their dens, often for days at a time.

Once the leaves are off the trees, stalking becomes even more difficult, since squirrels have virtually unlimited visibility. This is when a scope-sighted

.22 rifle has a big advantage over shotguns, because long shots are the rule rather than the exception. It's sort of like sniping, and an excellent test of a hunter's ability as a marksman. Serious hunters make certain they can hit what they shoot at, and accuracy is a part of a hunter's responsibility. A little practice on a range during the off seasons can go a long way in keeping this skill well-honed.

Hunters sometimes see squirrels run into the leaf nests they build for summer occupancy, but the temptation to shoot into these should be avoided. It's an unethical practice, because the nests may still contain young. Too, even if only one animal is present, there's a good chance it may die inside the nest and cannot be recovered. There's nothing wrong with throwing rocks or sticks at the nest in an effort to flush the animal out, and some hunters carry a sling-shot with which to lob rocks farther and more accurately. The idea isn't to penetrate the nest, only to use enough power to hit it or the tree limb beside it and put the squirrel on the run. If this can't be accomplished, the other options are to sit and wait for the squirrel to emerge, or move on and hope to find success elsewhere.

Hunters should also avoid shooting at a squirrel with its head protruding from a hole in a tree. If shot, it will almost always fall back into the cavity, and no hunter wants to lose game in this manner.

Two special aids that enhance a hunter's chances of success can be of value in both early and late season situations.

One is the use of a squirrel dog to locate the animals and keep them bayed until the hunter arrives. Nothing beats this approach when it comes to finding plenty of animals, and it's a lot of fun to follow a dog through the woods until it sniffs out a trail or spots a bushytail and gives chase.

There's no particular way to define these dogs except to say that the instinct to hunt squirrels may occur in any breed. Small mongrel dogs known as feists, or "fice," have always been popular, and while their ancestry may be varied and complex, it is likely that a good dose of terrier is somewhere in the lineage. Feists don't have the territory all to themselves, because the instinct to go after squirrels can show up in a broad variety of canines of all shapes, sizes and bloodlines.

There's a problem, however, in finding a squirrel dog. This wasn't the case when America was mostly rural, since every farm boy had what could best be called an "all-purpose" dog that would go after almost anything. All a hunter had to do to locate one was ask around at a country store. Usually someone would know of a youngster who'd be happy to act as guide and dog handler for a box of cartridges or a one-dollar bill. Today, with fewer small farms and farm families, finding a squirrel dog is a major coup.

The other aid—a squirrel call—is one to which everyone has easy access. Nearly every sporting goods store and hunting catalog features one or several models.

There's by no means a universal acceptance of these devices, and with good reason. Most are of little value except to entertain the hunter and give him the false hope of possessing a secret weapon. Too, the term call is somewhat misleading, since in almost every case the most that can be expected is to attract attention or get a reply. Squirrel language isn't well understood, but there's wide agreement that they do communicate vocally. The scolding sounds they make when angry or alarmed are easy to comprehend, but those

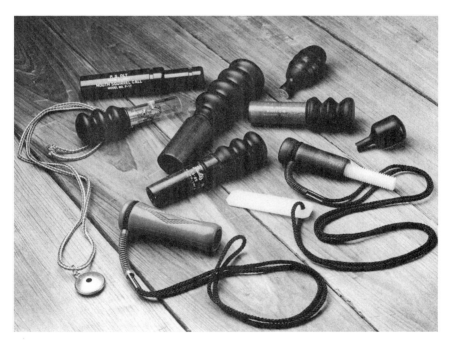

There are many kinds of squirrel calls on the market, including road calls and whistles; friction-type calls; and ones types, ones operated by percussion. Their effectiveness varies considerably.

who have listened carefully and extensively to "squirrel talk" know they make a variety of sounds, some of which are very subtle and can be heard only at very close range.

There are two notable exceptions. One is a call with an accordion-type rubber attachment that a hunter taps to supply air to a double reed system that operates on both expulsion and intake. With a little practice, a hunter can pro-

A whistle call helped draw this squirrel into range. Young hunter took gray squirrel with a Thompson Encore.

A few states have spring squirrel seasons, and one of the prime foods the animals seek during this time are mulberries.

duce sounds that are remarkably authentic—chatters, barks, and squeals—to which squirrels often readily respond.

The other is a whistle call that mimics the sound made by a young squirrel under attack by a predator. This triggers the maternal and paternal instincts in adult animals, and they expose themselves and begin scolding in protest. To make the scene more realistic, the hunter bends over a small sapling and swats the ground with its leafy top while calling. This is intended to represent the flailing of hawk or owl wings as they subdue their prey.

In the U.S., almost all squirrel seasons are set in the fall and winter months, but there are four states that offer spring opportunity: Missouri, Arkansas, Texas, and Oklahoma. This is traditional in these states, and called "mulberry seasons" in some places because of the squirrels' fondness for this fruit. They also feed heavily on the buds of some young trees, emerging fungi and other new growth. Wildlife officials claim that this early season has no adverse effect on the squirrel population. These animals, like many other rodents, don't have a spring, or one-time, mating period. They reproduce throughout the year, and young may be present in the nests at any time.

EQUIPMENT AND ACCESSORIES

The .22 rimfire rifle and the .410 shotgun are the most popular guns for squirrel hunting, and while it's rare that rifle calibers larger than .22 are employed except by blackpowder enthusiasts who prefer .32 caliber, it's not uncommon for shotgunners to use 20, 16 and 12 gauge guns. The sport has a following of handgunners, and again, the .22 rimfire is the favorite choice.

A hunter glasses for squirrels. Smaller gauge shotguns are generally preferred.

Some hunters like to go after squirrels with a muzzleloader, hunting them in the old-fashioned way, but a lighter, more compact modern version such as Connecticut Valley Arms squirrel rifle in .32 caliber is more practical than the original versions.

There's a choice between long rifle, long and short cartridges in both solid and hollow point styles. Solids will pass through a squirrel without great tissue damage, but the mushrooming hollow point usually has devastating results. The argument against solids is that they often cripple and allow the animal to escape and hide. This is true, yet for those hunters who prefer to shoot squirrels in the head, it makes little difference. The target is fairly small, and you either score a deadly hit or miss entirely. This is where a good scope can provide a big advantage, particularly in low light conditions. Very few hunters use shorts or long, since the long rifle cartridges provide maximum power and performance.

By getting within decent range of a squirrel and having a good scope and a steady hand, it's possible to make head shots that don't destroy meat, unless you happen to be one of the people who like squirrel brains. It's a greater challenge, and with such a small target, there's no danger of crippling: you're either going to hit or miss

As for shotguns, No. 6 or 7 1/2 shot is usually adequate, although some prefer No. 4s for big fox squirrels. Most important is getting within good killing distance, which varies according to shotgun gauge. The difference between the effective range of a .410 and that of a 12 gauge is as much as 20 yards. Too,

This pair of Bushnell Legend binoculars is light and compact, and perfect for spotting squirrels at a distance.

the 12 gauge sends out a much larger shot charge. Full choke barrels are what most hunters prefer, since a tight pattern is needed for a squirrel in a tall tree.

Hunting squirrels with other kinds of weapons also enjoys a certain amount of popularity. Blackpowder enthusiasts like to stalk them the "old-fashioned way" with muzzleloaders; handgunners go after them with .22 caliber pistols; and bowhunters find bushy-tails a special challenge.

Since stealth is paramount, footwear and clothing that facilitate quiet and unobtrusive movement should be chosen. Rubber-bottomed pacs are favorites of many hunters. They're soft, comfortable and lend good ankle support. Also, they're waterproof and ideal for traveling in wet and marshy spots. Moccasins and canvas walking shoes are okay, too, but not as practical in an all-around way.

Camouflaged clothing is preferable, especially when the pattern is matched up with the colors present in the woods at the time. Brushed cotton is the best fabric, because it's practically noiseless when it comes in contact with

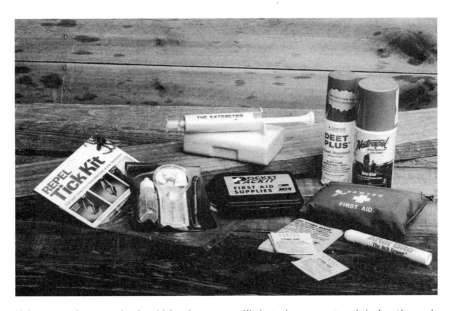

Ticks, mosquitoes, and other biting insects are likely to be encountered during the early part of the squirrel season, and minor accidents can occur. It's wise to be prepared for these annoyances.

leaves or twigs. A face mask and camouflaged gloves can help complete the "vanishing act."

Light, compact binoculars are a very useful accessory, particularly during those periods when the woods are barren of foliage. With this optical advantage, squirrel activity can be seen from a distance, allowing a strategy of

This mesh-type suit, pants, and parka repels insects, yet allows plenty of air flow. The suit is treated with insect repellent and can be used several times without recharging.

approach to be developed. They're useful at all times in locating squirrels that are hiding in foliage, lying outstretched on limbs, or tucked down into crotches of trees.

Binoculars can bring a lot of additional pleasure to the hunt. It's fun to sit and scan the woods, watching whatever activity interests you. Those who enjoy bird watching can view them in their natural surroundings instead of on a feeder. Hawks ordinarily patrol woods looking for squirrels and other rodents, and in early morning there's a chance to get a look at owls before they retire for the day. And few woods are devoid of chipmunks or some other kinds of animals to watch.

A day pack or fanny pack can be very useful for carrying other items such as insect and tick repellent, flashlight, compass, waterproof match case or fire starting kit, notebook and pencil, first aid kit and whatever else that's needed, including snacks or a lunch.

In places where squirrel season opens while the weather is still quite warm, mosquitoes and other biting insects can often make a hunter's life miserable. This plague can be virtually assured in the southern tier of states, and it's so severe in some low-lying areas that hunters avoid them until later in the season. Mosquitoes can easily penetrate the light clothing worn at this time of year, so unless repellent is applied all over the body, you're going to get bitten a lot.

There's a solution, though, and it's in a mesh-like outfit worn over the hunting clothes that's permeated with potent repellent. It provides head-to-ankle protection and makes it possible to go confidently into infested areas. The outfit can be worn over and over again, and when its potency wanes, it's a simple matter to recharge it to full strength.

Sitting under trees and watching for squirrels can sometimes be quite uncomfortable, especially when the ground is wet. To avoid this, take along one of the light, camouflaged cushions that can be attached to a belt. There's also an inflatable model that can be carried in the pack.

One other thing that can come in handy is a small camera. All that's needed to justify this addition is to think of all of the times you've wished you had one!

2

RABBITS AND HARES

Rabbits and hares are the most popular small game in North America, and historically they have supplied more sport and food for the table than any other animal. This isn't surprising, considering both their enormous reproductive capabilities, and the fact that there are over a dozen and a half species scattered throughout the continent from the Arctic to Central America. Of this number, all but two are native species. In the U.S. at least one variety can be found in every state, and in some instances there are several kinds present.

In most locations, rabbits and hares are regarded as highly desirable, since they furnish so much potential for hunters. There are exceptions to this, however. For example, in the West one type is regarded as a pest, making it one of the "fence-straddlers" that's both game and varmint. One of the exotic hares also occupies this category.

Except for some differences in size, weight and coloration, these animals are look-alikes, with long ears and powerful hind legs. Their diets are similar, also. They eat only vegetable matter—grasses, plants, berries, tree bark,

Cottontail rabbit.

shrubs, tubers and farm grains and produce—whatever is available in their home territories. Another characteristic they share is a preference for feeding at night.

Some rabbits and hares are burrowers, while others build nests above ground in dense cover such as briar patches, honeysuckle thickets, brush piles or woody tangles. They need all the protection they can get, since they have a host of natural enemies. Coyotes, foxes, bobcats, weasels, hawks, and owls prey on them, as well as house cats, dogs, and, of course, man. A talent for multiplying is their only salvation against virtual or total extinction. It's interesting to note that they're also able to manipulate population levels with what could be called "a built-in balance system" that automatically regulates the size and frequency of litters. Food availability is the key, so when lean conditions exist, fewer young are born, and the opposite is true in good times. Sometimes food supplies become super-abundant and population explosions occur that cost farmers millions of dollars in crop depredation. At such times it's often necessary to use drastic means to reduce the numbers.

Several of the species are broadly distributed, while others have restricted ranges. One variety is found only in small parts of two southwestern

Sinkholes, brush piles, or briar patches are havens that deserve investigating when rabbit hunting.

states where the dwindling population is subjected to very little gunning pressure. Some other types aren't important as game but are given plenty of attention by varmint hunters.

The Eastern Cottontail's extensive range encompasses all of the eastern U.S., most of the Midwest, and parts of the Southwest, mainly Texas, New Mexico and Arizona. It's plentiful in all of these regions, and more hunters seek this species than any other kind of small game. The color is gray-brown, sometimes with a white spot on the forehead and rusty hue around the nape of the neck. The ears are long and the feet whitish. Body weight is generally from 2 to 4 pounds. Several other rabbits share similar characteristics, and where ranges overlap this sometimes leads to confusion in identification.

During the past several decades, this cottontail has displayed a remarkable talent for adapting to the changes that have taken place within its range. The disappearance of small farms saw the passing of fence rows, fallow fields, briar patches and other features that were prime rabbit cover located in proximity to the agricultural crops that are their main food sources. The coming of large farm operations brought about the elimination of the cover, resulting in fields that are as bare as a table top. This meant that there were very few places of refuge adjacent to the crops upon which they depended for much of their food supply. Another factor entered into the picture: urban sprawl, which reduced suitable habitat even further. With hunting pressure constantly mounting, the cottontail was caught in a vise grip.

Unlike some other game animals and birds that can be managed with various kinds of manipulations, the cottontail cannot. This animal is a byproduct of agricultural practices. When the big changes in farming began taking place, rabbits had to "do or die," and they did it successfully.

The route they took to fit themselves into the scheme of things is a study in survival against pretty steep odds. Since cover was no longer available at places adjacent to the pastures and farm crops, the rabbits sought it elsewhere. This didn't mean they abandoned their food sources. They simply found secure spots that are often as much as a mile away. They come to the feeding areas after dark and return before daylight. Today, visiting cover remote from what were once hot spots is the best way to locate game.

One other adaptation should be noted. The "new rabbits" tend to be much less nervous and high-strung than their predecessors. They hold tighter and often let hunters or dogs pass within a few feet of them if they sense they're undetected. This adds new dimensions and more challenges to the sport.

The New England Cottontail is very similar in size and appearance to the Eastern Cottontail. The main distinguishing characteristic is a black spot between the ears. Woods and brush lands are the preferred habitat, and the range is limited to New England and south into the Alleghenies.

Marsh Rabbits like bottom lands, swamps, the edges of waterways and lakes. They have short ears and are dark brown above with a cinnamon-colored collar and a dark, short tail. They occupy all of Florida and lowland areas of Georgia, the Carolinas and Virginia.

The Swamp Rabbit, or "cane-cutter," is the largest of the rabbits, weighing up to 6 pounds. They are similar in appearance to the smaller marsh rabbit but have a thin white tail and rust-colored feet. Excellent swimmers, they take to the water without hesitation and can remain submerged with only their noses above the surface. Swamp rabbits are found in canebrakes, bottomlands and swamps in eastern Texas and Oklahoma and eastward to southern Illinois and northern Georgia. They leave their droppings on stumps or logs and eat them again when food is scarce. This is a primitive form of recycling, but one not unknown in other parts of the animal kingdom.

Cape or European Hares are exotics that were brought into New York in the late 1800s with the idea of establishing a new game species larger than the cottontail that would promote sport hunting. They eventually spread to other parts of New England and west to the Great Lakes region. They were also released in Pennsylvania, New Jersey, Maryland, Indiana, Illinois, Wisconsin, the Farallon Islands off California, Middelm Island off Alaska, and San Juan Island off Washington. At the last location they multiplied to the point of being serious pests. Their burrows, or warrens, were causing extensive damage. Large chunks of land were falling off into the sea, and the lighthouse on the island nearly collapsed before eradication measures were initiated. Thousands were poisoned, but some had escaped to a nearby island and the process had to be repeated there, also. Control measures continue today.

European hares are large animals that weigh from 6 1/2 to more than 20 pounds, with thick, kinky fur that varies seasonally from brown to gray above. The tail is black on top and white below. Their preferred habitat is open fields and woodlots, and they are fast and agile, making 12-foot bounds when running. Predators find them difficult to pursue and catch.

Snowshoe hare.

There is a German myth that claims the goddess of spring, Eostre, created the first hare from a bird. To show its gratitude, it began producing eggs during the annual Easter festivals. It was the birth of the Easter Bunny legend.

Snowshoe Hares are found in the East, but their broad range extends from eastern Canada all the way to Alaska, dipping into the U.S. in New England south to the Alleghenies, the Great Lakes region, from the Northwest south to California and in several of the Rocky Mountain states south to New Mexico.

This is also known as the varying hare because of its seasonal changes in color. In the summer it is dark brown above and grayish to white below, while in the winter it is white mottled with brown. The exceptions are in Washington and Oregon where the summer colors remain year around.

Snowshoe hares inhabit woodlands, and can run at speeds up to 30 mph. Their young are born with their eyes open and learn to run within a short time. Virtually every predator in the northern regions depends heavily upon the snowshoe hares for food. The population fluctuates from year to year, and once every decade the numbers become exceptionally plentiful. A sharp decline follows, causing lean years and dips in the predator populations, which are closely linked to the availability of this food source.

The tiny Pygmy Rabbit, which seldom weighs over 16 ounces is the smallest of all North American rabbits. It is gray or black above, with a dark tail and white spots on each cheek.

Pygmy rabbits inhabit sagebrush country and create burrow systems in which to live. Sage is the preferred food, and the strong flavor this imparts to the meat makes them undesirable as table fare. Their range includes southeastern Washington, southern Idaho, the southwestern tip of Montana, western Utah, Nevada, and a little slice of central California.

Another small species of the West is the Brush Rabbit. The fur is a reddish-brown flecked with black, and its ears and legs are short compared to other rabbits. Thick brush is the habitat in which they're most often found. The range is a narrow strip of the western parts of Oregon, California and the Baja.

Nuttall's Cottontail is also called the Mountain Cottontail because of its preference for the uplands. Medium in size, it is grayish-brown above, white below, and has black-tipped ears.

Its range includes central British Columbia; southern Alberta and Saskatchewan; eastern Washington, Oregon and California; and all of the Rocky Mountain states south to New Mexico.

The Desert Cottontail is found mostly south of the Nuttall's cottontail's range, but there is some overlap. It's a bit larger than its cousin, and has a bright rust-colored nape to go with the buff-brown-above, white-below body.

When available, grasslands are its favorite habitat, but in most of the places desert vegetation such as creosote brush is where it is found.

These rabbits are distributed from California to Texas, and north through the high plains to Montana and South Dakota.

Northern Hares inhabit the open tundra of the western and northern parts of Alaska. Adapting to their environment, they undergo a seasonal change of fur color. In the summer they're gray or brown above, white below and around the eyes, and have black ear tips. The winter coat is all white, but the ear tips remain black. Weights range from 7 to 10 pounds.

Despite the barren country it inhabits, the northern hare manages to forage successfully even throughout the winter when conditions are most severe.

No other native North American hare matches the Arctic Hare in body weight, which can reach as high as 15 pounds. It is almost identical to the northern hare in both summer and winter color phases, except that in some places it remains white all year.

Because of their range, which is northern Canada from McKenzie to Newfoundland, few people other than the Indians who inhabit this region get the opportunity to seek them. Their fur and meat are both valuable to the natives, and the other main predator is the arctic fox.

The long ears of the Black-tailed Jack Rabbit are what first earned it the name "jackass rabbit," which was eventually shortened to its present form. This is actually a hare instead of a rabbit, since the young are born fully furred and with their eyes open. Adult jack rabbits are sandy or buff-gray above, liberally sprinkled with black spots, and white below. The tail has a black stripe bordered with white. Weight is from 4 to 8 pounds.

The long, powerful legs help propel this animal at 30–35 mph in short bursts, with leaps of 20 feet. When pursued, it occasionally leaps high to survey the surrounding terrain for the best escape routes. It has the tendency to sit very still when danger threatens, apparently trying to decide what course of action to take.

The black-tailed jack rabbit is extremely unpopular with ranchers because it competes with livestock on ranges that have a minimal food supply. For this reason, they're regarded as varmints in many locations and are unprotected by game laws. They also can cause great damage to orchards and farm crops. In periods of high population levels they have been herded into wire enclosures and slaughtered by the thousands.

The native range of this hare is the western U.S., from California and Oregon, east to western Arkansas and Missouri, and south to Texas and into Mexico. It has also been introduced into other places such as Nantucket Island and Martha's Vineyard, New Jersey, and Kentucky.

White-tailed Jack Rabbits, also true hares, are most prevalent in the Midwestern and plains states, but they are distributed from eastern Washington and northeastern California, east to Wisconsin, south to Colorado, and north into Alberta and Saskatchewan. The lower part of their range overlaps with that of the black-tailed jack rabbit.

White-tailed jack rabbit

As its name suggests, this animal has a tail that is white both above and below. The body is brown and buff-gray above and white to gray below. Unlike its counterparts, its colors change with the seasons. In the northern part of its range, the long guard hairs drop out and are replaced by white ones. Further south, the summer browns become grayish. Its black-tipped ears and white tail remain the same throughout the year.

The white-tailed species also has long ears and legs that can move it along at speeds of 36 mph, with spurts of up to 45 mph. They're larger, too, with weights from 5 1/4 to 9 1/2 pounds. When pursued, it enters water without hesitation and is a strong swimmer. While this species is not welcomed by farmers and ranchers, its territory is smaller and has more plentiful vegetation, so it poses much less of a threat to crops and grasslands.

Antelope Jack Rabbits can make enormous leaps when fleeing predators, a feat which is responsible for their name. This jack rabbits' body is gray-brown above, the lower sides white, and the tail black on the upper side. The weight ranges from 6 1/2 to 9 1/2 pounds. Its long ears work as air conditioning and heating systems. In the summer they are held erect to allow body heat to escape more rapidly. In winter they are kept close to the body to retain warmth.

The range is south-central Arizona and southwest New Mexico, and they are extensively distributed in the arid areas of Mexico.

Closely related and very similar to the antelope jack rabbit, the White-sided Jack Rabbit is found only in the extreme southern part of Hidalgo County, New Mexico. The main difference between them is that the antelope jack rabbit has longer ears.

HUNTING METHODS

Of all of the kinds of rabbits and hares in North America, the cottontail is the one most popular with hunters, and considering the huge range the different varieties inhabit, it's no surprise. For example, in the Midwestern and plains states alone there are more harvested annually than all other species combined.

Because of the great diversity of geographic locations, habitat and types of terrain rabbits and hares inhabit, there are a number of different hunting techniques. However, the traditional and most used method of them all is simply walking them up.

There's nothing sophisticated about this approach, and it's the one used by a great many hunters to bag their first bunny. Also, it's democratic in the sense than no special skills or equipment are required. A farm boy stalking the cover with a slingshot has the same chance for success as the hunter toting an expensive double gun or fancy automatic. And although the different species inhabit a wide variety of geographic locations, habitat and terrain, they have the same basic instincts: to remain perfectly still and hope they are not spotted, or to bolt and run.

Walking up rabbits can be a solo endeavor or one shared by several people, but in either situation, one thing is extremely important:

Move s-l-o-w-l-y!

Rabbits are by nature very nervous creatures, and this characteristic can be used to great advantage by hunters.

The secret lies in patience. Rabbits will sit tight in cover and let hunters walk past them pretty closely as long as they keep moving. They think they're safe, so they don't budge.

The way to play on their nerves is to build tension. Take three slow steps, then stop and remain still for 20 or 30 seconds. This causes them to suspect they've been detected, and once they get fidgety, they're going to flush and make a dash for freedom.

This also works well for the hunter, because you're anticipating the rabbit's move instead of being surprised when it bursts out.

This slow stop-and-go strategy works well in all kinds of cover that can be easily walked through. It's especially effective in mechanically harvested cornfields where the flattened stalks provide excellent havens for rabbits and a perfect background for their natural camouflage.

This method is the one employed by those rare hunters who are able to consistently spot sitting rabbits. This is an enviable talent, and those who possess it have a great advantage in being able to actually be zeroed in on the cottontail before it makes a move. The trick is to look for the eye, not the body, since this is the one outstanding feature that isn't camouflaged. Armed with this particular skill, one can bag the rabbit with a slingshot or .22 rifle; and strange as it may seem, there are a very few hunters who can do it with thrown rocks.

One thing important to rabbit hunters is to maintain a line of movement so no one is lagging or ahead. It's also highly desirable that everyone wear a

Rabbit droppings are the best indication that there are animals in the vicinity.

blaze orange or brightly colored cap or vest (or both) so they can be easily seen in heavy cover.

As with most wildlife species, there are some variations in rabbits' behavior that are related closely to the places where they live. Whether it is in the midlands, swamps, desert, snowfields or mountains, there are particular kinds of ploys and strategies they have developed to outwit or confuse their enemies. Local hunters are aware of these, but it might take a visiting nimrod a while to recognize them.

All kinds of cover can harbor rabbits, and not necessarily in large quantity. Rabbits fare very well in suburban areas where minimal cover exists, and usually small plots of cover anywhere in the field are worth investigating. Sinkholes are especially productive, since they are usually located in or nearby agricultural fields. They can't be cultivated, so farmers usually allow them to grow up in vines, shrubs and saplings. They're hard for stalking hunters to penetrate, but they can literally be cottontail bonanzas. Sometimes these places are also favored by groundhogs, whose abandoned dens can become rabbit havens, which can tend to curtail hunting success.

Fallow fields are always good places to look for rabbits, and sometimes ones that are open are where they can be found on cold, clear days.

Fence rows, once standard on small farms, aren't as numerous now, but they're always worth working thoroughly, especially if they contain some substantial cover. They can pose a disadvantage to a single hunter, because more often than not the animals will go out the opposite side and deny the chance for a shot. With two or more hunters, both sides can be covered.

Brush piles are natural targets for hunters, and stomping around atop them will usually drive rabbits out. This won't work on some of the larger ones where it's hard to create enough commotion to inspire an exodus, but it's always worthwhile trying.

Briar patches and honeysuckle thickets can be very difficult if not impossible cover to work. Even if hunters can somehow wade through them, the rabbits inside often simply move around and don't emerge. Hunting these spots is a good way to get well scratched, frustrated and exhausted. They're better left for dogs, which will be discussed later.

There are times when rabbits can be found in what most observers would consider virtually no cover at all: open green fields of winter wheat or rye grass. The animals seek these places on clear, cold winter days and create very shallow depressions in which they can hunker down with ears flattened back and be nearly impossible to spot until one is only a few yards away. They do this in order to absorb the meager warmth of the winter sun.

Looking over the plot won't reveal anything, even in this very sparse cover. It requires walking over the entire field to jump the animals, because they will hold just as tight as in heavier cover. The interesting thing is that there may be a dozen or more cottontails sunning in a field no more than a couple of acres in size.

Abandoned or unkempt graveyards are great spots to check out, because they're almost always productive. Rabbits like these quiet havens, and perhaps it's because there's usually plenty of luxuriant vegetation. The same thing goes for the perimeters of any deserted structures, whether these are dwellings, barns or other outbuildings around which weeds have grown up. Rabbits also favor as refuges old farm machinery such as hay rakes or discs that have been left to rust, since they, too, are weed-infested and provide barriers against most predators.

Another of the prime cottontail haunts is a railroad right of way, many of which accompany lines that are no longer in service. There's usually good cover at these places. Ideally, one or two hunters can cover each side, and often a few miles of this kind of territory is all that can be comfortably handled on one hunt.

A sensible approach to this situation is to select a length of railroad bed and leave a second vehicle at or near the place where you plan to end the hunt. It saves a long trek back to the spot where you started.

The cover along ditches or creek beds is always worth working, since these are favorite sites for cottontails to hide in. They like to be near water, and usually there's vegetation available in these moist locations the year around. They're often within proximity to the fields in which they feed at night, and they are also very convenient travel lanes during the daylight hours.

Riverbanks sometimes provide top habitat, particularly in the form of canebrakes that are some of the safest cover rabbits can find. They're safe from winged predators, and the cane stalks are so thickly clustered that larger animals have trouble moving through them. The smaller and more lithe

The right of ways along railroad tracks are prime rabbit habitat, since they often lie adjacent to agricultural fields.

cottontails can manipulate these mazes with great skill and speed. In addition, by being adjacent to the water, they can swim to safety.

It was explained earlier that changing agricultural practices have caused a shifting of rabbit populations to new habitat areas. Because of this, hunters should no longer depend on finding them in what were once obvious places. Many locations that used to pay off are now nearly barren of cottontails, and unless you understand what has happened, the outlook may appear bleak. To change this perspective, begin seeking out cover well away from old standbys and sample some of the cover spots you once would have bypassed.

The cottontails have changed, so you must do the same.

A light snowfall can be a hunter's delight, since it allows rabbits to be tracked to their hideaways following a night of feeding and frolic. Of course, tracking is commonplace to those who hunt the snowshoe and arctic hares, but it's a method unknown to hunters in most of the southern states.

Perhaps the most satisfying and exhilarating rabbit hunting method is with a good pack of beagles, because having these energetic, short-legged bunny chasers along can add a wonderful dimension to any hunt. The mere sight and sound of these tenacious hounds on the trail of a rabbit is a special thrill, and even if a shot isn't fired, you return home with the feeling of a very satisfying day in the field.

Beagles can bore into cover that defeats hunters, so this means more rabbit potential is investigated. Too, they cover a lot more ground, and since cottontails have the tendency to run in a wide circle, hunters can stand near the place where the rabbit was flushed and be fairly sure it will come back past them sooner or later.

Hunting with beagles increases the enjoyment of the hunt, and boosts the chances for success.

This isn't true of the swamp rabbit, which is more likely to select a straightaway path and follow it until the beagles are out of earshot. "Swampers" have longer legs than cottontails, and they're considerably faster, so they often evade both dogs and hunters. Their other method of evasion is to enter the water and swim away, and in the water they can easily outdistance a dog. Their smaller cousin, the marsh rabbit, has similar characteristics, so they show up in hunters' bags a lot less frequently than cottontails.

There are numerous breeds of beagles, some of which date back to early America and beyond, and it is undoubtedly a point of pride to own a pack of purebreds. However, most hunters are more oriented toward performance, and many "home-grown" packs do exceedingly well in the field.

In the West, jack rabbits are more or less what individual hunters consider them to be, regardless of how they're classified by the states. To farmers and ranchers, the jacks are considered varmints because of the damage they do to crops and grasslands. On the other hand, sport hunters find them challenging targets, and the younger animals are quite palatable on the table.

Due to the nature of the terrain, much of the hunting is done with rifles, which may range from .22 long rifles to .220 Swift, according to the shooter's ambitions. There are also many handgunners who like to hunt jack rabbits with the high-tech, scoped models chambered for high-intensity cartridges. Finally, stalking them in the open country with shotguns can be a real test of skill and reflexes. A flushed jack rabbit can put a lot of distance between itself and a hunter very rapidly!

Naturally, there are numerous variations in hunting methods where all the different forms of rabbits and hares are concerned, but they're too many to discuss here. Besides, it would lessen the fun of discovering them firsthand.

EQUIPMENT AND ACCESSORIES

Most rabbits are taken with shotguns and, according to the situations and conditions in which the animals are being sought plus the skill of the hunter, there's no gauge that can be counted out as a possibility.

The 12 gauge is probably the most-used of all, since it has the greatest range and tosses the largest shot pattern. Both of these factors can be of great importance at times. The 20 gauge also has a large following, and this is mainly because of two things: first, it's a lot lighter than the 12 gauge (and dur-

Smaller-gauge shotguns are okay for rabbit as long as their range capabilities are taken into consideration. This hunter bagged his cottontail with a .28 gauge gun.

ing a day in the field, this can make a big difference); second, by using a gun chambered for 3-inch shells, it compares favorably with the 12 gauge. The 16 gauge is a great compromise, but sadly, this "in-between" gauge is gradually disappearing from the scene.

Of the smaller gauges, the .410 (which is actually a caliber) and the 28 gauge are both fine choices for beginners, since they have light recoil and give a young shooter confidence in gun handling. There are also skillful hunters who prefer to use these smaller gauge shotguns in order to add more challenge to the sport.

The use of high brass or low brass shells depends on several things, including the size of the animal and the ranges at which it will be shot. No. 6 is a good all-around choice, since it's large enough to be effective on all rabbits and hares. Smaller shot are okay, but you put a lot more pellets into the meat than is necessary, and this can be a minor problem at the table.

As for rifles, a pump or automatic .22 long rifle model is plenty enough for cottontails, and the addition of a low-power scope increases accuracy. Similarly, a scope-sighted .22 caliber handgun can be effective in the hands of a

The Thompson/Center Kit Gun features both .410 shotgun and .22 long rifle barrels, and is made in both adult and youth models. It offers a rabbit hunter the opportunity to switch in the field.

Long-barreled .22 helped this hunter take five nice hares.

trained shooter. The more powerful center-fire .22s aren't recommended for this species.

Footwear is an important item, and it should be keyed to the kind of terrain in which you'll be hunting. Sturdy leather boots with a cleated sole are fine for dry or rocky country, while the rubber-bottomed pacs are versatile and practical under almost all conditions. Hunters slogging around in marshy places after swamp or marsh rabbits will find knee-high rubber boots very advantageous. Wearing a light pair of cotton socks under the heavier boot socks will help keep the feet drier and more comfortable. Tip: It's a good idea to carry along an extra pair of socks in case the others get wet or too damp from walking.

The kind of obstacles rabbit hunters usually face means that tough outer garments are a must! The coat should be roomy and water repellent, with an ample game bag in the rear, and pants that are double-faced on the legs and seat. Many hunters in the southern states where temperatures are moderate wear only a vest with shell loops and game bag instead of a coat. The hat should be red or blaze orange for personal safety, and a pair of gloves that allow the trigger finger to be free help to keep hands from being scratched while passing through briar patches or thickets.

3

OTHER ANIMALS

Although squirrels, rabbits, and hares are by far the most popular of the small game animals, there are a number of other species that offer hunters additional opportunity. The degree of interest shown in them may vary according to the range and distribution, but several have enthusiastic followings in places where they're most numerous. Too, each represents a separate challenge in terms of methods and tactics used to bag them.

Putting them in the small game section is an arbitrary decision, since the way they are classified by the various agencies isn't always the same. In different locations they may be designated as game, furbearers, unprotected species or varmints.

For example, opossums and skunks are unprotected in Wisconsin and Michigan, while they're listed as game animals in Tennessee and Kentucky. Not infrequently, a species will occupy more than one of these categories, and if so, hunters may seek it for different purposes, whether for meat, fur or fun. Two of the species, raccoon and skunk, are common carriers of rabies, and

Raccoon.

when afflicted they often show no fear of man. This is often mistaken for "friendly" behavior, and children are especially vulnerable because of having been given false impressions of wild animals through television and story-books.

What should be made clear is that it's best to avoid handling any wild animal. It has also been proven that armadillos carry the organism responsible for leprosy, but this doesn't appear to be a threat to humans.

RACCOON

The Raccoon, with its bandit's mask and ringed tail is one of the best known of the small game animals, principally because of the apparently "cute" behavior it displays. Depictions of them in cartoons have helped enhance this image. One common misconception is that raccoons wash their food to be sure it's clean, but this isn't correct. They do it to examine what they're holding to be sure it contains no undesirable or foreign objects. There's nothing hygienic about it.

Raccoons are omnivorous, eating almost everything, and crayfish are a staple in their food supply.

Contrary to the general public's perception, game managers and hunters alike know the raccoon to be one of the most cunning and destructive of the small game species. If its habits were more widely known, the "cute" reputation would no doubt suffer.

Classed as a carnivore, or meat-eater, the raccoon is actually omnivorous. The range of its diet is very broad, including songbird and waterfowl eggs and fledglings; squirrels, muskrats, young beavers and other small mammals; chickens and other domestic fowl; crayfish, salamanders, snakes, turtles and their eggs; insects, grubs, berries, nuts and numerous farm vegetable crops, particularly corn. They also boldly roam populated areas and forage for whatever they can find. The raccoon has extremely nimble fingers that can pry the lids off garbage cans, open latches and refrigerator doors, and turn doorknobs. Dog and cat food left outside is a favorite target for these nocturnal ramblers.

Raccoons occupy various kinds of habitat, but river bottomlands, lakeshores and wooded areas along streams are preferred. These are locations where many of the food items they consume are found. Dens are usually in hollow trees, but sometimes they are in abandoned animal burrows. The fur of raccoons is valuable and the meat is quite palatable.

'Coon hunting is a nocturnal activity, and the most important ingredient for success is a pack of well-trained hounds. They're essential in the chase, and the aesthetic aspects of listening to them baying during the chase is where most of the pleasure and satisfaction is gained. Without this element, interest in the sport would diminish sharply and probably die out.

There's a long and colorful history of the various types of hounds that have been used to pursue raccoons. While generally referred to as tree hounds, no particular breed or mixture can claim exclusive rights to the territory. However, there are certain bloodlines recognized as superior that have been carefully preserved over the years. The buying and selling of 'coon hounds involves big dollars, and a pack of dogs can be worth a small fortune.

The hunting method is relatively easy to explain. Dogs are released at a selected location, and the hunters usually don't get underway until the dogs give vocal indication of hitting a hot trail. As with rabbits and foxes, this is another sport where the sound of the hounds in pursuit of the quarry is as exciting as the culmination of the hunt.

Once a trail is struck, hunters follow up. In most cases, this means striking out into the darkness and plowing through briars, swamps, thickets, creeks

Raccoons are usually hunted at night with dogs, and it can be a rough-and-tumble kind of operation.

and various other obstacles. It's tough going, but it's a part of the game 'coon hunters relish. They're a dedicated bunch, and even if they end the night limping, scratched, bleeding, wet and without game, they're smiling. Non-hunters would view this activity as totally mad, but the hunter knows that 'coon hunting is a sport designed for the hardy. The weak need not apply!

When the dogs tree a 'coon, the hunters spot it with a light. Mature animals are harvested and the young ones left alone.

'Coon-on-a-log contests were once a popular spectator sport for hunters until the practice came under pressure from outside groups that saw it as inhumane. A raccoon was shackled to a floating log and the dog pack was released to go after it. The ensuing battle was usually ferocious, since the raccoon had solid footing and the dogs were swimming. The outcome was usually predictable due to the overwhelming odds. The results are often different in a hunting situation when the two animals meet in the water one-on-one. Raccoons are at home in the water, and their usual tactic is to wrap their legs around a dog's head and drown it.

The best rifle calibers for raccoons are the .22 WRF Magnum, .22 Hornet and .222 Remington, although if the pelts are not a consideration a shotgun with high brass No. 4 loads will do the job very satisfactorily. Knee-high rubber boots and tough, briar-proof clothing are basic necessities. Other important items include a powerful spotlight or headlight and a smaller flashlight for use while traveling through the woods and checking equipment. The lights, which attach to a gun barrel, are also very useful, since this leaves both hands free when shooting and directs the light precisely on the target. It's also

A 'coon hunter uses a headlight to see while moving through the woods, and to spot animals that are treed.

The right footwear is important when 'coon hunting, and this can include knee-high rubber boots, rubber-bottomed pacs or waterproof leather types.

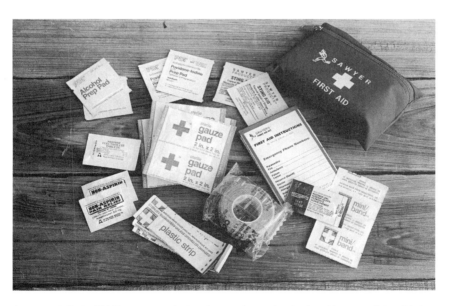

A compact first-aid kit can come in handy on a 'coon hunt when there are lots of briars and barbed-wire fences as obstacles.

All of these emergency items are worthwhile having along on night hunts, since some-times a hunter ends up in trouble or in unfamiliar territory.

wise to carry a compact first aid kit to treat injuries suffered by both hunters and dogs. Another handy accessory is a fire starter kit, since on chilly nights it's nice to be able to warm up and dry out between chases or after the hunt.

Raccoons are unprotected in some places, and the hunting seasons vary greatly where they are classed as game. Special dog-training seasons are also sometimes in effect during which no animals can be harvested.

Predator calls can also be used to hunt raccoons, but this will be covered in the varmint section.

The raccoon is widely distributed from the southern edge of the Canadian provinces all through the U.S. except for some of the Rocky Mountain states and parts of Utah and Nevada.

There are two other members of this family. One is the Ringtail or Civet Cat, which is found throughout the Southwest and California, in southern Oregon, parts of Nevada and Utah, and south through Mexico to Central America. Unlike the raccoon, its fur and meat aren't valuable, but man is a principal predator. The other, the Coati, inhabits the southeastern parts of Arizona and New Mexico, southwestern Texas, all of Mexico and into the woodlands of Central America. It also has no commercial value.

A light day pack is easy to carry and ideal for including all of the items needed for a night hunt.

OPOSSUM

The Virginia Opossum is the subject of many folk tales and jokes, notorious for its "grin" and its habit of feigning death when threatened. This is the only marsupial, or pouched animal, in North America. The opossum is grizzled gray above, and white below, with whitish face, slender snout and a long, scaly tail. Its size is similar to that of a large house cat.

Opossum

Open woods and overgrown areas are favored habitat, but it isn't unusual for them to invade urban areas to raid garbage cans. In the wild, they're not discriminating and eat carrion, snakes, frogs, salamanders, small mammals, berries, fruit, and various crops, particularly corn. They inhabit hollow logs, abandoned burrows, caves or practically any site that offers shelter. 'Possums feed mostly at night, and great numbers of these slow-moving, clumsy creatures are run over by vehicles on the highways. Their taste for road kills may have something to do with this. They become what they're looking for.

Opossums are sought for both fur and meat, the latter of which is considered a delicacy by some people. Because of opossums' affinity for carrion, many hunters prefer to capture them alive, then hold them in pens and feed them a diet of vegetable matter to clean out the digestive tract and improve the meat. In recent years the fur has been of little value, so the species is given less attention by trappers. Hunters use dogs to find and tree the animals, but sometimes in the fall when persimmons are ripe, hunters go afield seeking them with only lanterns or flashlights. Persimmons are a favorite food of other animals, particularly raccoons, which no doubt gave rise to the old Southern ditty:

'Possum in a 'simmon tree,
Raccoon on the ground.
Raccoon say "You son-of-a-gun!
Shake them 'simmons down!"

The opossum's range has expanded since the first settlers arrived, and includes most of the eastern U.S. except Maine, northern Michigan and northern Minnesota; southwest to Colorado and parts of Arizona and Texas; and in the coastal areas of the West from British Columbia to California.

A .22 rimfire rifle is sufficient for opossums, and if they are shaken out of a tree or cornered on the ground, a stick will put them in their state of faked death and they can be picked up and tossed into a burlap sack.

ARMADILLO

The Nine-banded Armadillo enjoys the colloquial nickname of "'possum on the half-shell," but this is a misnomer. While the two species are somewhat alike in appearance, and both are candidates for the title, "King of the Road Kills," they're not at all related. Each occupies a separate order, and in

Armadillo

the U.S. each is the single member within that category. The shell is tan to black, with sparse hair sprouting between the plates. It has a small head and a long, tapering tail.

Spanish conquistadors first encountered this strange-looking creature in Mexico and called it "little man in armor." It's an apt name, since it's the only living mammal with bony shell plates.

Armadillos may be on the move at anytime during the night or day, scurrying around and rooting in vegetation for food or digging the burrows in which they live. Their main diet consists of insects, grubs, worms, salamanders, and crayfish, eggs of birds and reptile and carrion. They appear slow and clumsy, but are surprising fast and agile.

While not seriously pursued by hunters, these animals are quite good to eat. The meat has the flavor of pork or chicken. Tourists to some of the areas where they are found are offered baskets, bowls and handbags made from the shells. Although armadillos roam during the day, most hunting for them takes place at night when they're most active. They often supplement the bag of 'possum and 'coon hunters. Unlike the opossum, which plays dead when cornered, the armadillo rolls up into a tight, nearly impenetrable ball.

Armadillos migrated into the U.S. from Mexico and have spread widely through the southeastern states. They were deliberately introduced into Florida in the 1920s, and now their range extends from that state through the southern parts of Georgia, Alabama, Mississippi, Louisiana, Arkansas, Kansas, and much of Texas. Since armadillos don't hibernate and can't survive extended periods of freezing weather, geography will eventually establish a range limit.

SKUNK

The Skunk is in a family that also includes weasels, otters, badgers, minks, and fishers, and there are four species represented.

The most widely distributed of these is the Striped Skunk, which is found in almost all of the U.S. and in many of the Canadian provinces. The Eastern Spotted Skunk's range includes Minnesota and South Dakota and south to Texas and Louisiana; and, in the East, Illinois and central Pennsylvania south to Mississippi, western South Carolina, and Florida. The two other species, Hooded Skunk, and Hog-nosed Skunk, have limited range in the southwestern states.

Skunk

Skunks are omnivorous and eat small mammals, bird eggs, amphibians, grubs, insects, berries, and a wide variety of vegetable matter. In urban areas, skunks cause lawn damage when rooting for insects, and occasionally they will take up residence under houses. They're also notorious for invading campsites.

Mostly nocturnal, skunks spend the daylight hours in hollow logs, burrows abandoned by other animals, crevices or brush piles. They do not hibernate, but they may remain dormant during periods of severe weather.

Although a gentle, harmless creature by nature, the skunk is a formidable adversary when threatened. It is equipped with anal glands that contain a potent musk that can be sprayed at intruders, which is usually sufficient to deter further action. The smell is distinctive, and few people are unacquainted with it, either as a result of personal contact or through literature or movies. In the earlier western films, the skunk's nickname, polecat, was commonly applied to unsavory characters.

The pelts of skunks are valuable, so it has been a prime target for trappers over the years. Small game hunters have sought them for the same reason, usually with the assistance of a dog. Earlier in the century, there were skunk hounds bred and trained specifically for locating and baying the animals. The hunter would follow up and check the pelt to see if it was worth taking. Since fur with too much white had little value, such animals were usually left unharmed.

Hunters are sometimes sprayed in unexpected encounters with skunks, an experience that is never forgotten. The intensity of the odor at close range is sufficient to cause vomiting. The best scent neutralizers are tomato juice or ammonia, followed by washing the skin with a strong carbolic soap.

MUSKRAT

Both the Common Muskrat and the Round-Tailed Muskrat are generally thought of as animals sought primarily for their fur, but there are those who like the meat and hunt them for this purpose alone. In weight they range from 1 1/4 to 4 pounds.

While the round-tailed type is found only in southeastern Georgia and throughout the Florida Peninsula, the common muskrat's range is extensive in North America. They're found everywhere except the arctic regions of Canada; parts of California, and a few southwestern states, including Texas; and Georgia and Florida. Not particularly selective when it comes to the types of water they inhabit, they take up residence in creeks, rivers, canals, marshes, ponds, and lakes.

Muskrats feed primarily on aquatic vegetation, but will on occasion eat fish, clams, mussels, and crayfish. In the wild, their main enemies are raccoons and mink, which open up muskrat houses and devour the young.

The meat of muskrats, often called "marsh rabbit," is good eating, and at one time it was fairly popular and was sold commercially. One of the best ways to harvest muskrats is to locate yourself near a stream, river or lake that you know they inhabit and pick them off with a scope-sighted .22 rimfire or .22

Muskrat

WRF Magnum rifle. They move about during daylight hours, and all that's required to bag them is patience and the ability to hit a swimming target.

NUTRIA

This larger version of the muskrat was introduced in Louisiana from South America in the 1930s in an effort to boost the fur market. Eventually it spread into surrounding states. It was also introduced in Washington and Oregon, some Great Plains states, Maryland and New Jersey.

Nutria is similar to the muskrat in most ways except for size—it can be up to five times as big. Because of this, those who find it good table fare get some hefty portions when they bag one. These animals become pests when populations are high, causing damage to stream banks and overbrowsing to vegetation along waterways.

BEAVER

Anyone familiar with American history is well acquainted with the part beavers played in the opening of new routes of travel and centers of commerce as the westward movement continued. Because of their valuable fur, they were the prime goal of trappers who continued to probe into new and unexplored areas in search of them. It was a relentless campaign, and trapping continued unregulated until it resulted in the animal's disappearing from much of its original range. Since that time, beavers have become well reestablished all over North America, and in many places their numbers are greater than anytime in the past. The only places devoid of them are California, Nevada, and Florida.

Beavers feed primarily on the bark of trees, but they also eat tubers and other vegetation growing close to the water areas they inhabit. They have become classified as varmints or pests in some places because the dams they build flood out valuable commercial timber and croplands. To combat this problem, there are now professional beaver exterminators for hire, a stark contrast from the days when they were so highly prized.

A good example of this exists in Manitoba, Canada, where beavers have greatly increased in numbers and have wreaked havoc throughout the province. They have built dams that have flooded highways and grain fields, and in addition, felled the poplar trees farmers plant as windbreaks. While the principal amount of damage has been in Manitoba, beavers have also invaded the suburban areas in heavily populated southwestern Ontario, damming small creeks and streams, which have led to the flooding of stands of trees.

With fur prices too low to give trappers incentive, the government has spent hundreds of thousands of dollars in beaver control measures, but to little avail. Blowing up dams is only a temporary deterrent, since they can rebuild them in a very short time. Officials say beavers are winning the battle, so it's anybody's guess as to what the future holds.

Other than man, the only natural enemies of the beaver are the bear and wolf, neither common enough throughout their range to make inroads in the population. Beavers can weigh up to 80 pounds, and a big adult is more than a dog or coyote can handle.

The meat of beavers is very good, and the fatty tail is considered a delicacy in the northern parts of the continent.

PORCUPINE

Nearly everyone has seen or heard of the Porcupine, an animal unique in North America because the sharp quills it carries as defensive weapons.

Slow-moving and nonaggressive, this animal has few enemies except for a few carnivores that have the ability to get at its soft underparts without getting peppered with quills. The porcupine's range is Canada; Alaska, and most of the western U.S.; northern Minnesota, Michigan and Wisconsin; and New England south to New York and Pennsylvania.

The porcupine's diet consists of leaves, tree bark, clover, and various kinds of woodland vegetation. It is also fond of salt and is notorious for chewing wooden and leather goods that have absorbed human perspiration.

There's not much incentive for hunters to go after porcupines unless they happen to be lost or incapacitated and truly desperate for something to eat. The animals are easy prey, since all it takes to kill them is a sharp blow on the nose. All things considered, potting them from a distance with a .22 rifle might be a better choice of action. The Indians used the quills for decoration and also ate the meat.

MODERN VARMINT HUNTING

There have always been birds and animals in this country that were considered varmints, so it's also accurate to say that there have always been varmint hunters. Youngsters potting away at English sparrows or starlings with a BB gun, or shooting rats and other small rodents with a .22 rifle qualified, as did the farmer who considered all hawks "chicken hawks" and who also had numerous animals such as weasels, foxes, skunks and the like with which to contend. And there are few hunters who haven't taken shots at some varmints during their time in the field.

Early varminters used the large bore rifles that were traditional for all kinds of shooting at that time, and it wasn't until the late 1800s that efforts were made to get away from the big, heavy, hard-kicking models. Breech-loading rifles with self-contained cartridges were fairly new to the scene, although none was much smaller than .40 caliber. The departure from this standard was initiated by a small group of target shooters in the New England states who began to experiment with some small-caliber cartridges intended for use as "pest guns" both on the range and in the field.

The main "pest" that spurred the effort was the woodchuck, which can logically be considered as the "father" of the movement. This region was heavily populated, and hunting opportunities were limited, but those hungry for more action discovered that the highly abundant woodchucks offered great potential for additional sport. The problem was that most landowners weren't eager to have hunters on their property banging away with big bore guns, and it became obvious that the only solution was to create rifles that were less noisy and better suited for the purpose.

By today's standards, the cartridges that resulted aren't impressive, but they led to recognition of varmint hunting as a sport and the new pest rifles' stature as a separate class of firearms. What came about were the .22 WCF (Winchester center fire), .22/15/60 Stevens, .25/20 or .25/21 Stevens, developed around the turn of the century, all of which were small bullets matched up with large cartridge cases that could accommodate the kind of black-powder charges needed to propel the bullets at high velocities. The performance of these cartridges was enhanced by matching them up with the single-shot schuetzen rifles produced by Stevens, Winchester and Ballard that were the favorites of target shooters. Not surprising, these were the same people who became the first dedicated varmint hunters.

The early cartridges had several limitations, one of which was that the small bullets had a very poor trajectory. They were okay up to about 100 yards, but after that the rate of drop was enormous. Little was known about bullet design and how it influenced velocity and trajectory and how this in turn affected accuracy. Also, target shooters' inclination to stick with black powder as a propellant was a disadvantage. Smokeless powder was available, but favored by reloaders. When smokeless powder was accepted in the early 1900s some interesting cartridges showed up that were to have real impact on subsequent developments.

The most impressive of these newcomers was the .22 Savage High-Power introduced in 1912. It had greater muzzle velocity than its predecessors, and the performance was much more suitable for shooting at longer ranges. Because of poor marketing strategy, it never had a chance to prove itself to the public.

Another that had great potential was the 6mm Lee Navy, a cartridge originally designed for the 1895 Lee rifle that was used for a time by the U.S. Navy. Because hunters' thinking still referred more to target shooting than varmint hunting, this hot round wasn't given much attention. The irony of this is that

According to their size and the distances at which they're shot, varmints are hunted with everything from .17 caliber pellet guns to cartridges like the Viper .22 Long Rifle and larger.

only minor changes were necessary to convert the original Navy case into the .220 Swift, still one of the greatest varmint cartridges ever.

The era of what can be called modern varmint hunting began in the late 1920s with the appearance of the .22 Hornet. There is irony here, also, because the developers of this cartridge, Townsend Whelen and G.L. Wotkyns, used the obsolete .22 WCF case along with jacketed bullets and smokeless powder to produce what is still regarded as a phenomenal little cartridge for medium-range varmint work.

One of the principal differences between the .22 Hornet and its predecessors was that it was the first to be promoted strictly as a varmint round, and this faced most manufacturers with a problem. Varmint hunting interest wasn't what they considered to be substantial enough to warrant all-out promotion, so they chose a sort of sit-back-and-wait attitude. At first, most .22 Hornets were the result of rechambering of the Model 1922 Springfield .22 rimfire rifles, but the most exposure was through the Model 54 Winchester and Savage's Model 23D.

The main forces that brought the public's attention into better focus on varmint hunting were the writings and promotional efforts of Col. Townsend Whelen. At the time he was a contributing editor for *Outdoor Life* magazine and very well respected in the shooting community. Helpful also was the growing awareness by the public of the constantly shrinking seasons and bag limits for most game species, which fueled their desire to find other shooting outlets. Varmint shooting was the only choice for a year-around sport, and from that initial recognition of the facts it has shown a steady increase in interest and participation.

At this point is it important to mention that the evolution of varmint hunting to the level of sophistication it has reached today has been due in large part to the contributions of the bench rest shooters. It has been this group of highly skilled and talented individuals upon whom varmint hunters have always depended for improvements in the design and performance of both cartridges and rifles.

It has been a good marriage, because bench rest shooters enjoy the challenges presented them, and the results have pushed varmint hunting higher in terms of respectability. And once varmint hunting proved itself to manufacturers, they became very cooperative and quite willing to produce the rifles and ammunition that showed special promise.

Not long after the .22 Hornet appeared on the scene, two of the country's leading experimenters, Jerry Gebby and G.L. Wotkyns, were looking toward much hotter cartridges that would attain previously unheard-of velocities. Their work led to Winchester's introducing the legendary .220 Swift in 1935, with an astounding 4,100 fps muzzle velocity. Yet what should have been the establishment of a permanent place in the realm of varmint shooting became a morass of controversy, misunderstanding and misinformation that doomed it to be virtually shelved for many years. For instance, one prominent writer claimed that the Swift cartridge "followed no rules in reloading," and that the slightest irregularities in the load would cause pressures to rise to astronomical heights. Another writer leveled the charge of excessive barrel wear. Neither assertion was true, and even though nothing in the field compared with the Swift's performance, the adverse publicity prevented its real potential from being realized by shooters.

It should be noted that all the while, bench rest shooters were constantly experimenting with various "wildcat" cartridges. Many of these never became commercially available, yet each usually made a contribution of some sort and helped advance the technology. The same still goes on today, although almost all of the possible options have been exhausted. There is one prominent exception which will be mentioned shortly.

There's no possible way to list all of the persons associated with the avalanche of advancements that occurred during this period. However, in addition to those already mentioned, J.B. Smith, Harvey Donaldson, Hervey Lovell, Leslie Lindahl, Lysle Kilbourn and P.O. Ackley are some others who were particularly significant.

The Europeans had also been at work developing new cartridges, but those they produced were far better suited for game larger than varmints, since there are few small animals to hunt in those countries. The best known of the European cartridges were the 5.6X61 Vom Hofe Super Express and the 5.6X35R Vierling. They also used the .22 Savage High-Power round, which was known as the 5.6X52R. The British .240 Apex was a hot 6mm cartridge that would have been all right for varmints, but such creatures were of no interest there. None of these cartridges generated any interest whatsoever in America.

There were other commercial calibers produced during the 1930s that were of some importance but not of lasting popularity. Among these were the .218 Bee, .219 Zipper, .25/20 and .32/20. Marlin currently produces a lever gun in all of these calibers except the .219 Zipper, and ammunition remains available.

A true "sea change" occurred in the sport of varmint hunting in 1950 when Remington introduced its terrific .222, with a 3,200 fps muzzle velocity, because it was the first of a succession of super-accurate varmint rifles that would raise the sport to a much higher level and attract new hunters by the thousands.

The .222 quickly became the most popular varmint cartridge of all time. Because it was entirely new, rather than an update or reconfiguration of a previous cartridge, it represented a refreshing change.

Something else: the event marked the entry of Remington into the varmint field, which until this time had been dominated by Winchester. Also, the .222's instant popularity wasn't lost on European gunmakers, who were eager to take advantage of the varmint hunter's appetite for this new caliber. It was this recognition that resulted in the magnificent Sako, Krico and other fine rifles showing up on the American market.

There's little doubt that the .222 Remington brought large numbers of new varmint and bench rest shooters into the fold. The .222 was highly accurate and comfortable to shoot, devoid of the kind of muzzle blasts produced by some of the other calibers. It was popular both on the target range and in the field. Warren Page, who was the shooting editor for *Field & Stream*, gave the .222 an enormous amount of publicity, since he was deeply involved in bench rest shooting as well as varmint hunting. A later version of this cartridge, the .222 Magnum, had a brief history, mainly because it didn't comfortably fit into the existing pattern of varmint calibers.

The next important step by Remington was the .223 cartridge, 3240 fps, which is by far one of the most successful rounds of all time. It was manufactured for both civilian and military use, with the latter being classified as 5.56 ammunition. The .223 is excellent for long-range varmint hunting and has been very competitive with the .222 in capturing the hearts of bench rest shooters.

In terms of muzzle velocity, the .222 and .223 are almost identical, so performance doesn't give either an edge. However, the easy availability of less-expensive military ammunition has definitely had a bearing on shooters' deciding between the two at point of purchase.

The next two cartridges to appear were the .243 Winchester and .244 Remington. Both are 6mm caliber, and except for the long-ago Lee Navy cartridge, they were the first 6mm rounds to be seen by most Americans.

Winchester's .243 was the first out of the gate, and with a 3,500 fps velocity, it was second in this category only to the .220 Swift in conventional rifles, which in 1935 Winchester announced as having an astounding 4,100 fps muzzle velocity. Weatherby had a .257 Magnum, but only that company loaded ammunition for it.

It didn't take long for the .243 to gain popularity, and as more manufacturers began producing rifles chambered for this cartridge, the surge of interest mushroomed.

Remington's .244 followed, and while plenty of competition developed between the two rounds, it was the .243 that eventually triumphed. One of the reasons is that Winchester went after both the varmint and deer hunter in their sales campaigns, but another was that hunters were in love with the sleek, beautifully crafted and accurate Winchester Model 70, and Remington's Model 722 simply couldn't divert their attention sufficiently to make it feasible to continue production. Its life span was only five years.

Other calibers bit the dust soon after these 6mm rounds appeared. Manufacturers ceased making rifles chambered for the .257 Roberts, .250 Savage and .220 Swift, and although two of these would later reappear, they were absent for quite a while.

One of the "oldies" in the crowded field of wildcatting was the .22/250, an extremely fast and efficient cartridge dating back to 1930. Bench rest shooters prized this highly accurate cartridge, but amazingly, the firearms manufacturers ignored it until the mid-1960s when Remington adopted the round and began producing ammunition. While Browning had the first .22/250 rifle on the commercial market, Remington was soon in competition with two chambered for it: a Model 700 and the superb 40-X target rifle. This satisfied both field and bench rest shooters, and soon they were in wide use. The result was that several other manufacturers, domestic and foreign, began building .22/250 rifles.

This finally established the .22/250 in the place it always belonged: in the same league with the best performing varmint cartridges of our time. It has accumulated a huge following, and rightly so!

The .220 Swift is also back, but still not on a scale that's anywhere near what it deserves to be. The Swift is the top-stepper of the varmint cartridges, with a better than 4,100 fps velocity. On the commercial market, it's available from Remington in its Model 700 and from Ruger in both the classic No. 1 and Model 77, the latter of which is an extremely fine varmint rifle by anybody's standards. A couple of manufacturers supply commercial loads.

Weatherby produced two varmint cartridges, the .224 Magnum and the .240 Magnum. Both are fine performers, and the .240 is capable of taking down animals larger than varmints. Despite the excellence of both of these

The Ruger No. 1 in .220 Swift gives the varmint shooter the ultimate capability that can be obtained with commercial cartridges. The bullet zips along at more that 4,000 fps.

rounds, neither enjoys the high profile exhibited by most of the other varmint calibers. That's because the rifles are quite expensive. Many shooters dream of owning a Weatherby but settle for something they can better afford. However, Weatherby's newest addition to the field, the Mark V Super Varmint-Master (SVM), can be considered as the company's first true varmint rifle. Available in a repeater or in single shot, the SVM weighs only 6 1/2 pounds. The major selling point, however, is that unlike most Weatherby rifles chambered that way for their magnum cartridges, the SVM is available in .223 Remington, .22–250 Remington, .220 Swift, .243 Winchester, 7mm-08 Remington and .08 Winchester.

An interesting varmint cartridge that still may someday enjoy more popularity than it has attained so far is the .17 Remington, which tosses a tiny 25-grain bullet out of the muzzle at better than 4,000 fps. There have been a number of .17 caliber wildcat cartridges around for a long time, some of which gained considerable recognition, but no commercial rifle or ammunition was produced until the .17 Remington appeared in 1971.

This little caliber had lots going for it in terms of speed and accuracy, because it compared favorably with the .22/250 in some respects. It was also an efficient and quiet rifle for woodchucks and crows, and the small bullet was sufficient to do a thorough job on either of these. The one disadvantage was that due to its weight, it didn't fare well in wind.

The Weatherby .224 Magnum is a popular varmint rifle with long-range capabilities.

Somehow, varmint shooters never embraced the .17, so it has been virtually relegated to the wings. The nice thing is that's it's still being produced, and perhaps it will be better received by a future generation of shooters.

Shooters who own a .30/06 rifle and have a yen to use it on varmints can do so with the Remington's Accelerator cartridge, which is nothing more than a .22 bullet encased in a plastic sleeve, called a sabot, the size of the bore. When fired, the bullet and sabot separate shortly after leaving the muzzle and the .22 bullet goes on its way. Though not capable of pinpoint accuracy, the Accelerator is okay for larger varmints like coyotes.

It's been explained that experimenting with wildcat cartridges has been the major force in advancing target and varmint shooting to its present position. This isn't carried on as avidly as it once was because so many avenues have already been explored. However, there are still plenty of target and varmint shooters who prefer the wildcats to the calibers available on the commercial market. Too, as with almost everything else in the field of science (and target and varmint shooting are definitely in that arena), new and exciting things continue to occur—and the future may hold even more.

Today, the most popular of the wildcats is the .22 CHeetah, a cartridge designed by Jim Carmichel, shooting editor for *Outdoor Life*, and Fred Huntington, founder of RCBS, which makes reloading tools. The round moves out at the astonishing velocity near 4,300 fps, and performs ideally for long-range target and varmint shooting. Two major custom gunmakers, the Shilen Rifle Company and Wichita Engineering, now produce rifles in .22 CHeetah.

The new .17 HMR (Honady Magnum Rimfire) is an exciting addition to the world of rimfire cartridges, because no other has achieved the kind of accuracy and flat trajectory it delivers. Combining the ballistic efficiency of Hornady's V-Max bullet with the powerful new propellants available today creates a cartridge that delivers the kind of velocity and flat trajectory that is beyond most shooters expectation of rimfire accuracy. Providing honest 200-yard performance, the .17 HMF is ideal for plinking, varmint shooting, or squirrels and rabbits.

The cartridge evolution has been accompanied by equally impressive developments in the firearms built to accommodate them. The sophisticated, ultra-accurate rifles available today are enormously advanced from the early pest guns and are capable of delivering the high-intensity rounds precisely in extended range varmint or target shooting.

It didn't begin that way, of course. At the outset, the major emphasis was on cartridge development rather than accuracy. Typically, varmints were shot at fairly close range, so pinpoint accuracy wasn't of great importance. Ironically, some of the early experimental cartridges had potential far beyond the rifles' capability.

What brought attention to the importance of accuracy was the "bench rest connection," those varmint hunters who were also target shooters. They knew that a cartridge was no better than the firearm from which it was delivered, so their focus was on this aspect of performance.

Bench rest rifles were heavy and cumbersome, with long barrels and stocks that were little more than big blocks of wood intended to supply solid support. Initially, it was believed that the main keys were the bullet and the barrel. If the bullet was right and the barrel straight and true with smoothly finished lands and grooves, a marksman's eye could do the rest.

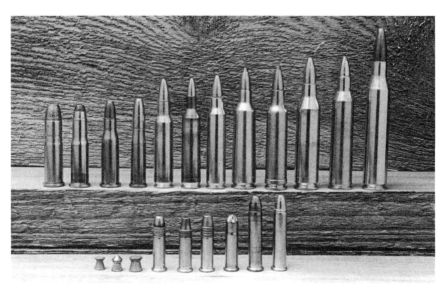

A variety of varmint ammunition. Top, left to right: 32–20 Winchester, .26–20 Winchester, .218 Bee, .22 Hornet, .222 Remington, .17 Remington, .223 Remington, .22–250 Remington, .224 Weatherby, .243 Winchester, .220 Swift, .25–06 Remington; bottom, left to right: .177 precision match pellet, .177 pointed field pellet, .22 precision match pellet, .22 long rifle solid, .22 long rifle hyper-velocity, .22 long rifle hollowpoint, .22 long rifle bird shot, .22 Winchester Magnum hollowpoint, .22 Winchester Magnum full-metal jacket.

At fairly short ranges, this premise held water, but as shooting distances were increased it became obvious that a lot more factors were involved. One of the first discoveries was that bullet performance was greatly influenced by how the rifle was fitted into the stock. It was learned that a "floated barrel," one that did not touch the wood, was more accurate, thus the science of properly bedding the rifle into the stock was born. Likewise, if the action wasn't properly seated, minor twisting could influence bullet flight. Today's excellent synthetic stocks allow gunmakers to accomplish bedding to a degree of perfection not possible with wood, and although the aesthetics aren't the same, the bottom line — performance — can't be argued.

These changes came about gradually. As varmint hunters paid more attention to the matter of accuracy, their bond with the bench rest shooters continued to solidify. While much of the credit goes to the bench rest shooters, it wasn't entirely a one-way street; each was making important contributions, and combining forces and sharing information accelerated progress.

Of course, improvements in all aspects of bench rest and varmint rifles were, and are, continuing. Once it was recognized that each of the rifle's components represented an area of specialization, advancement was accelerated. In the custom and commercial fields there were craftsmen and engineers concentrating solely on particular parts: barrels, actions, triggers or stock design.

The varmint rifle as we know it today evolved from this collaboration. The kind of firearm practical for field use varies considerably from what is necessary for precision target shooting; yet combining forces and utilizing the products created by advanced technology are constantly creating better "recipes". As a side note, there is a NASA connection: some of the knowledge of ballistics gained by shooters aided in NASA's space flight program, and materials developed for this program have in turn been useful to gunmakers and shooters.

Winchester and Savage were the first manufacturers to get into the varmint rifle field once the .22 Hornet appeared, but it was some time until they began to fully understand that it was bolt action rifles that were by far the best for long range shooting. Both made some lever action models that didn't do justice to the cartridges for which they were chambered. Before commercial rifles were available, most were custom conversions from military models, and bench rest guns were all custom made.

A selection of varmint outfits: left to right, Savage 112PV in .22–250 and Simmons 6X–20X scope; Winchester Model 70 Sporter in .22–250 and Bausch & Lomb 6X–24X scope; Winchester Model 70 Varmint in .223 and Leupold 3.5X–10X scope; Ruger Varminter in .223 and Leupold 6.6X–20X scope; Remington Model 700 Varmint in .22–250 and Redfield 4X–12X scope; Ruger Model 77 Mark II in .243 and Leupold 2X–7X scope; and Weatherby Mark V in .224 and Weatherby 2X–7X scope.

The picture remained essentially the same for quite a few years, but after World War II there was an upsurge of interest in varmint hunting. This got the attention of other gunmakers, and the competition stiffened. Remington made a major move into the field, and with the success of its .222, became extremely high profile.

Other than these three, many other manufacturers have been in the varmint rifle business through the years. Of the domestic companies, the names that are best known are Ruger, Browning, Weatherby, Dakota, Colt, Mossberg, Marlin, Kimber, Harrington & Richardson, Stevens, Ithaca and Smith & Wesson. Some of these firms are no longer in business, and a couple of others have dropped their rifle lines.

As for the foreign gunmakers, the Belgian firm, Fabrique Nationale, was one of the first to enter the U.S. market. Later, the superb Finnish Sako rifles took varmint shooters by storm, and Sako actions were widely used by other manufacturers. Others followed, of which Krico, Anschutz, BSA, Mannlicher, Kleinguenther, Husqvarna, Mauser, Charles Daly, Heckler & Koch and Interarms are the most familiar.

The quality of many of the commercial firearms is first rate, and some are of superior quality, but a varmint hunter seeking the ultimate in a rifle will end up doing business with a custom gunmaker. There are several outstanding companies in the U.S., and their products are without peer anywhere in the world.

A custom rifle represents the finest in technology, engineering, and handcrafting; but more than that, it is created specifically for the client in terms of weight, balance, stock material and design, trigger pull, recoil management and ornamentation. The difference in the feeling of mounting a custom rifle and one off the rack in a sporting goods store is similar to that of trying on a tailor-made suit after always having worn ones bought in a department store.

There are many custom gunmakers, most of which use the very best component parts available to assemble their rifles; but a few build the entire product themselves. Also, custom makers can chamber a rifle for whatever the client desires. There are still many shooters who prefer particular wildcat cartridges, and custom rifles are the only solution other than conversions.

While it's logical that small bore rifles will always dominate the varmint shooting field, it's worthwhile mentioning that there's also limited potential for big bores in the overall picture. Varmints are occasionally hunted with cartridges designed for game as large as elephants, such as the .458 Win. Magnum, .404 Jeffreys, .416 Rigby and .375 H&H Magnum. Other big boomers like the .340 Weatherby Magnum, .300 H&H Magnum, .338 Winchester and .45/70 Government aren't strangers to the sport.

It may not make sense at first glance, but there are valid reasons why these heavy-duty cartridges are used. One is that big game hunters usually have little opportunity to use their large bore rifles. Shooting varmints provides a way to keep in practice and feel comfortable handling this type of firearm. Whatever kind of varmint they go after is much smaller than the game they will be seriously hunting, so if they can consistently score on them, they can feel confident of their marksmanship. Another is that some hunters just enjoy firing the heavy kickers occasionally, and varmints are a greater challenge and more fun than plinking away on a target range.

A contrast in varmint cartridges. On the left, a .416 Rigby; on the right, a .224 Weatherby Magnum.

Incidentally, this big bore varmint shooting isn't restricted to rifles. Many handgunners are involved for the same reasons.

Finally, it doesn't take much thought to come to the conclusion that you can't over-gun any varmint, and that there's little difference in the results of hitting a prairie dog or a woodchuck with a .220 or a .458. Both are devastating.

A majority of serious long-range varmint shooters do their own reloading. There are several reasons for this, and while economy is surely one, the ability to experiment with different bullets and powder charges is also of great importance. Reloaders can also work up new loads of their own design, and this helps to determine the ones that perform the best at various ranges and for miscellaneous kinds of varmints.

Reloading can add much to enjoyment of either varmint or target shooting, but it is something that requires great discipline and attention to detail. Matters of weight and measurements are of extreme importance, and often a gram of powder can put a load over or under the prescribed limits.

There are numerous companies that manufacture and market reloading equipment, as well as all of the necessary component materials. Also, there are several dependable manuals that fully describe standard and alternate loads for all commercial and many wildcat cartridges, and reloaders should refer to all of them when checking out information on any load in order to see if there are alternate formulas.

Expense isn't an obstacle, because basic reloading tools can be purchased at a quite moderate price, and these sets are best for the beginner. Learning from the bottom up is beneficial and helps a handloader to better understand the principles and limitations involved.

Cartridges and rifles have been explained, but there's a third element without which long-range varmint and target shooting wouldn't be possible: the telescopic sight.

No matter how well a cartridge performs, or how accurately a rifle can deliver the bullet, long-range shooting is impossible without optical assistance in the form of what is commonly referred to as a rifle scope. Put simply, this is a device that compresses the distance between the shooter and the target through magnification, providing the opportunity for precise bullet placement. Like Sam Colt's famous revolver, it's an "equalizer" that allows both young and old eyes to see the target on the same plane and to focus clearly on the target.

Telescopic sights have been around for a long time, although not in the form we are using today. The earliest scopes had long, thin tubes that extended almost the entire length of the barrels, which at that time were pretty long. These rudimentary optics were employed mainly by the military in this country and abroad. During the Civil War, snipers on both sides used telescopic sights. After the conflict, target shooters adopted scopes, but even though the optics were very good and their performance quite creditable, the instruments were delicate and not sturdy enough for hunters to use in the field. Varmint and small game hunters relied on open or peep sights.

Hunting scopes began showing up on the American market around the turn of the century. Most were produced by German and Austrian firms, of which there were several; but two in particular—Zeiss and Kahles—are still quite familiar to target shooters and hunters. These first scopes were similar in appearance to those being produced today, and some were of surprisingly fine quality. What isn't obvious is that they weren't fogproof and waterproof, didn't have coated lenses, and lacked the sophisticated internal adjustments now considered standard. The magnification range was from 2X to 5X, with the same basic choice of reticles: post, duplex, cross hair, and dot.

Even after this kind of scope became available, varmint hunters didn't flock to buy them, choosing instead to continue to use open and peep sights. Two things came about in the early 1930s that turned some heads. First, a German-American technician named Rudolph Noske created a rifle scope with

This Remington 40XB with a Lyman 10X Super Targetspot scope is still considered one of the finest bench rest combinations.

internal adjustments and long eye relief, solving two of the shooters' most nagging problems. Second, a Texan, Bill Weaver, began producing a line of high quality, modestly priced scopes that the average hunter could afford to buy. It was revolutionary, because until that time, mostly well-heeled sportsmen owned scopes. Most important, the cost of Weaver scopes and mounts made all manufacturers, domestic and foreign, compete on the low rather than the high end of the price spectrum.

This didn't eliminate the high-ticket scopes, of course, because bench rest and varmint hunters serious about the ultimate in accuracy at long range still look toward the finest models available. Two early favorites were the 15X Lyman Super Targetspot and the Unertl 12X Ultra Varmint scope, which some still consider to be the best in their class. Yet the advantages that today's state-of-the-art scopes offer pretty well overshadow anything produced in the past.

For instance, internal adjustments, coated and fog-proof lenses, and compact design are standard on most models, but that's just the beginning. Beyond that are features that provide the shooter all kinds of special advantages. One of the most significant is the variable scope that can change magnification with the twist of a dial. A variety of choices exists, with the 1.5X-6X, 2X-7X, 3X-9X the most popular, but 6X-24X models are also available for ultra long-range shooting. Too, there are scopes with built-in rangefinders and trajectory compensators that take some guesswork out of zeroing in on a target. And it's no problem finding the kind of reticle that suits the best, since there are many from which to choose. If you like, you can also have a laser scope, or one with just a lighted dot.

Firing the Remington 40XB in the field using a sandbag on a car top as a rest.

As rifle-scope technology improved, so did that devoted to spotting scopes and binoculars. Both are very important items on the range and in the field. They're made more versatile by window mounts for locating targets from the comfort of the car seat, and special brackets that permit mounting binoculars on a tripod make it much more comfortable to scan with the higher-power glasses.

Yet, although rifle scopes offer shooters a definite advantage, the real test of marksmanship still lies with the individual. Simply attaching one to a rifle doesn't ensure an instant improvement in shooting skills. A lot more is involved, and while no single formula works in all situations, there is a basic plan to follow.

Place the rifle on a sandbag or other solid rest with the target 50 yards away. Bore sighting will help put the first shot on paper. Next, by manipulating the vertical and horizontal adjustments, a few more shots should bring the point of impact to the desired place. Follow this with a 100-yard test using a target with the appropriate size bull's eye. By checking the ballistic information for the cartridge, it can be determined where the bullet should be striking

There are many high-quality rifle scopes on the market, and the most popular are those with variable power range.

Removing the bolt is the first step in the cleaning process.

Since lead and copper accumulate in the barrel, it's necessary to use a good solvent to remove it.

Run the patch through the barrel several times to be certain that all of the residue is wiped away.

at 100, 200 or more yards, according to range capability. Of course, this will apply only to the cartridge being used, and a change in any of its characteristics—powder charge, bullet weight, and style—will alter the trajectory pattern. It's an early hint as to how many variables exist, and how complex things can become later.

One thing important to recognize is that the performance of a rifle depends on the skill of the person handling it. No matter how excellent the equipment, unless the shooter can place the cross hairs or dot precisely on the target and squeeze the trigger properly, it can serve no benefit.

Equally as vital to precision shooting is keeping the rifle or handgun bore and mechanism spotlessly clean. In many cases, according to the loads being used, it's necessary to run a swab through the bore after every few shots. Lead and copper accumulations in the barrel have a very significant effect on bullet performance, and a full complement of cleaning equipment is a must on the range. The same applies for shooting in the field when a lot of rounds are going to be fired. There are cleaning kits designed for every situation and circumstance that range from pocket size to large, deluxe models.

Pistols need the same attention as rifles. The Harris bipod on this Thompson/Center Contender allows it to stand up by itself.

This Rusty Duck cleaning kit has everything needed for cleaning guns in the field.

By comparison with the older solvents and lubricants, the modern versions make gun cleaning a pleasure, and they are enormously more effective in keeping the equipment in top shape.

Going into detail about all of the aspects of varmint shooting that have been touched upon would be impossible. There's a vast amount of both technical and practical information too voluminous to include. For those wishing to delve deeper, there's no better source available than Jim Carmichel's *Book of the Rifle*, which is recognized as the standard reference on the subject and the most complete book on all types of shooting ever written.

5

WOODCHUCKS

Today's varmint hunters owe a great debt of gratitude to the woodchuck, or groundhog, because it is the animal on which the sport of varmint hunting was founded. Starting with the "pest guns" of the early days, the woodchuck has been what could be termed the official unit of measure for cartridge and rifle development. It is also what helped define this type of hunting as a distinct and separate shooting sport and elevate it to its present sophisticated and high-tech status. Today it remains the most popular of all varmints, and despite all of the attention it has received over the years, still one of the most abundant.

The woodchuck is another of the rodents in the Sciuridae family that includes about five dozen species in areas from the Arctic to Mexico, and although its range isn't that broad, it still occupies a lot of territory. Woodchucks are found all across Canada and into east-central Alaska, and southward into northern Idaho. In the eastern half of the U.S., they occur from northeastern

Woodchuck

North Dakota south to Arkansas, and from New England to western North and South Carolina, and northern Georgia and Alabama.

There is only one woodchuck species, but due to the color variations that occur in the different locations they inhabit, they're called by other names. In the high mountains of the West, woodchucks are known as whistlers or marmots, the latter of which is a separate species. They also have local nicknames such as "pasture pigs" or "pasture poodles."

The extent of their range also indicates the versatility of the animal in adapting to a wide variety of conditions that includes everything from sea level to high mountain altitudes, and from southern climes to the deep-freeze temperatures of the far North. The same goes for habitat. Although most woodchuck hunting is done on farmlands, they also are found in areas where no agricultural practices occur. They're just as much at home on mountain slopes, in woods, and along streams or rivers, although in these places the population levels are lower than where crops are grown.

Woodchucks are heavy-bodied, short-legged animals that may attain weights of up to 14 pounds. Their fur varies from a yellowish brown to almost black, and is grizzled with white-tipped hairs. The undersides are a much lighter color. They are burrowers, using their forelegs to loosen the soil, and kicking it out with their hind legs. Generally solitary creatures, about the only time two adults are together is during the mating period. The young are born in late April or May, with from four to six in a litter, and the female is entirely in charge of rearing them. At about 2 months of age they disperse and are on their own.

The dens woodchucks create typically have several entrances, with tunnels from 30 to 40 feet in length and sometimes extending to depths of 30 or more feet. Centrally located in the network of tunnels is a large chamber that contains a grassy nest. There will also be chambers for food storage, and for defecation, the latter being sealed off once full.

Woodchucks almost always hibernate during the entire winter in the northern part of their range, but sometimes they are seen moving about even in the snow. Usually this is because their sleeping chamber wasn't excavated deeply enough below the frost line to keep them warm, or their body fat wasn't sufficient to maintain body heat. Such animals seldom survive.

In the South, though, woodchucks remain only semi-dormant and are likely to emerge anytime there's a warming trend. Since states in this latitude don't have winter-long snow cover, some kinds of food are always available for the off-season snackers.

The characteristic of hibernation is why this wild animal is one of the best known to the general public, even in parts of the nation where it isn't found. This is because of the popularization in America of an old European legend that claims that if on February 2 (Groundhog Day) the woodchuck emerges and sees its shadow, there will be six more weeks of winter. This superstition is said to have been introduced by immigrants who settled in the South. However, the town of Punxsutawney, Pennsylvania, where the ritual is staged with a pet animal, "Punxsutawney Phil", has long captured the focus of attention on this make-believe, scheduled appearance. It gets plenty of media exposure each year but has even less chance than the human weather forecasters of being correct.

The woodchuck is mostly a vegetarian that feeds on grasses, clover, alfalfa and other succulent plants, although it will also eat insects, small birds, and mice. It has a great fondness for grain crops, and the damage several of these animals can do to a field of young corn and soybean plants can make it appear that areas have been mowed. In places near cities where much truck farming is conducted, woodchucks invade fields and enthusiastically go after cabbage, lettuce, cauliflower, beans, peas, and root vegetables. Even a few animals can make heavy inroads into these crops in a short time, so the farmers class them as major pests. Woodchucks create similar havoc in domestic gardens.

Before most of the large timber tracts in the eastern U.S. were cut, the populations of these animals were minimal. Once agricultural practices were begun and an abundance of food became available, a great increase in their numbers occurred. Due to this environmental change, there are likely more of them present today than when the Pilgrims arrived.

More than just ravaging of farmland crops can be attributed to the woodchuck. Livestock can suffer broken legs by stepping into their den entrances, and while the instances of this may be very infrequent, the possibility of its happening is enough to encourage landowners to be rid of them. One threat that is real is having the ground above heavily tunneled areas collapse under the weight of tractors or other heavy farm machinery and causing broken axles or other costly mechanical damage. Also, in places where concentrations of woodchuck burrows occur, they can cause sinkholes to develop.

Hay fields are prime woodchuck habitat. The animals are easy to spot once the fields are mowed.

A woodchuck's home range is usually from 50 to 100 acres, depending on the kind of territory they occupy. In locations away from agricultural activities, they often wander over larger areas in order to find sufficient food. To ensure their safety on their longer trips, they develop a series of alternate dens that can be used for emergency purposes, whether it is a threat or bad weather. However, woodchucks generally don't settle in at any place that doesn't have a fairly generous food supply within a short distance of their dens. If this should dwindle for some reason, they will move on to "greener pastures."

While woodchucks spend the principal amount of their time either on the ground or under it, they can climb trees with considerable dexterity; and despite their stubby legs, they're quite good swimmers. When gathering food, they can carry rather large amounts in their pouched cheeks, dashing back to their dens every now and then to deposit the booty. Most of the activity occurs in the early morning and late afternoon hours. During the heat of midday, they usually loaf in the cool confines of their burrows.

At locations where there are lengthy "dog days"—periods with extremely high temperatures, woodchucks may virtually disappear until the heat onslaught diminishes. These "siestas" may last for as long as several weeks, during which time hunters are better off staying at home near the air conditioner watching baseball games.

When cooler early autumn weather finally arrives, woodchucks finally emerge and begin a feeding binge that will add the layers of fat needed to sustain them through the coming winter. This increased activity makes the fall months especially productive for hunters, and it's usually the best time of the year to be in the field. The animals are also engaged in another important activity: preparing their dens for the long winter ahead. If the one they're occupying isn't just right, they either renovate it or go to work on digging another that will be suitable.

Man is the most important enemy of the woodchuck, but coyotes and foxes also prey upon them. Hawks can't handle anything but young woodchucks, which don't come out of the den often; when they do, the mother keeps them close to the entrance. In places where there are eagles, these birds are capable of snatching up full-grown animals. Too, since woodchucks often like to feed alongside highways, many fall victim to vehicles.

Not many hunters eat woodchucks, and they're missing an enjoyable culinary experience by not doing so. The meat is very tasty, and when properly prepared can be as desirable as most small game animals. Predictably, young ones are the best.

The other foes of woodchucks are mainly fleas and ticks, both of which are capable of creating infestations severe enough to either drive the animals from their dens or cause them to become too weak to survive.

Although the focus of attention is mainly on the economic downside of the woodchuck, its lifestyle also has benefits. The burrows they create become dens for other animals, including cottontail rabbits, skunks, opossums, foxes and raccoons. At one time woodchucks were protected by law in Pennsylvania because their burrows served as havens for rabbits during the winter. Rabbits were prime game for hunters, and the state was interested in their survival because of the license revenue that resulted from heavy participation in seeking these animals.

A great change has come about since that time. The law was rescinded, and today Pennsylvania may actually have more woodchuck hunters than any other state in the nation.

Getting permission from landowners to hunt woodchucks seldom is a problem, mainly because, unlike game animals, these are critters they want to be rid of. They consider that the varmint hunter is doing them a favor, saving

Pastures are good bets when looking for woodchucks like this.

them both time and trouble. As long as a hunter conducts himself properly, there's usually a standing invitation for return visits. Good relationships are valuable, and as a hunter explores more territory and becomes acquainted with more farmers and landowners, more places become available to shoot woodchucks. It's smart to have plenty of "aces in the hole," just in case!

Hunters in the western U.S. are outside the woodchuck range, but an animal that's quite similar in appearance and habit provides plenty of action for them.

The Yellow-bellied Marmot, or Rockchuck, is a smaller version of the woodchuck, with brownish-yellow upper parts, a yellow belly, light to dark brown feet and a pair of white spots between its eyes. The weight is from 5 to 10 pounds.

The yellow-bellied marmot's diet includes grasses, succulent plants, and berries. Although it is a burrower, sometimes its den is found in rock crevices, rock shelters, and under rock piles. This animal forms colonies and inhabits mostly mountain regions up to elevations of 12,000 feet. It enters into hibernation at different times, disappearing as early as August in some locations. Emergence is usually in early spring, and mating takes place shortly afterward.

The yellow-bellied marmot's range includes British Columbia, Alberta, Washington, Oregon, California, Idaho, Montana, Wyoming, Utah, and Colorado. It's important to know that this animal is host to the tick that carries Rocky Mountain spotted fever.

Another species, the Hoary Marmot, also has the nickname, Rockchuck, but its range is mainly in British Columbia, Alaska and the Yukon, with some found in the high country of northern Washington, Idaho, and Montana.

This burrower is quite different in appearance from the yellow-bellied species. It is slightly larger, attaining weights of up to 20 pounds, and has a silver-gray upper body and a whitish belly. There are distinctive white and black spots on its head.

Because of the remote areas most of the hoary marmots inhabit, they aren't seriously sought by varmint hunters, but native Indians of the region use their pelts for parkas, and also like to eat them. Their other enemies are wolves, bears, and eagles. There are several subspecies, none of which is of significance to hunters.

HUNTING METHODS AND ACCESSORIES

Because woodchucks are found in such a wide diversity of habitat, the ways to go about hunting them cover everything from the simple to the sophisticated. To illustrate this, compare the farm youth prowling pastures with an ordinary .22 rifle, looking for a 50-yard shot, to the fellow with a .220 Swift with a 6x-24x scope zeroed in on a target too distant to see clearly with the naked eye.

In between these examples lies a broad array of hunting tactics and techniques, and weaponry that encompasses everything from primitive to high tech. You can indeed "pick your poison" when participating in this sport!

Terrain has much to do with the choice of methods. There's a big difference between shooting over flatland agricultural fields and pastures and hilly or mountainous turf, and also at places where the animals are in secluded niches in the woods or in spots close to human habitation. A proficient hunter will have capabilities of handling any of these challenges.

Since the woodchuck is so closely associated with long-range, precision shooting, this is the best-known strategy for hunting them. To accomplish it, the hunter seeks out groundhog habitat, scouts it thoroughly, then returns to set up at a place where the territory can be observed with binoculars and spotting scopes at whatever distance desired from the burrow openings. Usually, the location selected will provide the chance to bag several animals, and the hunt may be an all-day affair.

This is the kind of circumstance in which the best of equipment and accessories can be put to test. Ideally, conditions approximating or duplicating

Woodchucks are not hard to spot in soybean fields when the plants are still fairly short. After that, they can move about and not be detected.

bench rest situations can be achieved: distances can be accurately measured and point of bullet impact observed.

There's nothing rudimentary about such setups, and in many instances the major objective is not to bag woodchucks but to experiment with bullet capabilities and performance. That's how the sport began, and this aspect of it has never changed. Of course these shooter/technicians have contributed immensely in the development of the varmint hunting tools available today, and they continue to do so.

There are field shooters who don't go to such extremes, but the methodology is somewhat similar. Once a woodchuck-laden field is found, they pick a spot where the most territory can be watched over, then settle in and wait for the action to begin. One of the best ways to find places with plenty of animals is to drive around back roads and stop to glass every pasture or open field. Sometimes the animals don't have to be visible, since groundhog holes are easy to spot from a distance, proving that the animals are present.

The best times to scout are in the morning before the sun gets too high, or from mid- to late afternoon. Spending some time finding places where

The light Weatherby .224 Magnum is perfect for off-hand shooting, since it doesn't have a heavy barrel.

there's lots of activity will result in establishing an inventory of dependable spots to visit. Once permission to hunt at each is obtained, there's no problem in finding action.

No matter what the hunting methods, keeping a record of each excursion can prove valuable. Noting the date, time of day, weather conditions, ground cover (crops, pasture, etc.) and number of animals taken will be useful for future reference in planning trips. All are important influences that should be considered when developing hunt plans.

The "walk around" approach, in which the hunter sets out on foot to locate the quarry is probably the most challenging in an overall sense. A lot of different skills are required to be successful. This is a hunting style that works well in undulating or rough terrain that can't be looked over from a distance. It's a slow, deliberate kind of stalking in which it's necessary to stop frequently and survey the surroundings. The idea is to spot the woodchuck before it sees you, and then sneak up as close as possible before shooting.

Sometimes this is a fairly easy matter, but there are instances when some extra effort and caution must be exerted. A good example of this is trying to bag woodchucks in soybean fields when the plants are about 18 inches high. Groundhogs can't be seen when on all fours in feeding position, but every now and then they stand up to check for danger. Once an animal's location is determined, a hunter can belly-crawl between the rows until close enough for a sure off-hand shot. It's best to be at least three rows to either side of the one in which the foraging is taking place. It's a game of chance in some respects, because the time comes when the hunter has to rise up for a peek, and if the woodchuck does the same thing simultaneously, the opportunity is missed. This is a tactic that also pays off well for blackpowder enthusiasts, bowhunters and handgunners.

One of the most overlooked of areas of potential lies in what might be termed as "ultra-close" shooting. This entails eradicating the varmints around, and sometimes in, farm buildings, particularly ones in which hay or grains are stored. However, no structures are exempted as possible home sites, including residences.

The extent of damage done by the animals in such situations can be extensive. The most serious occurs when woodchuck burrows undermine foundations, which can cause all or parts of buildings to collapse. Too, living in proximity to the farmer's garden, they can have a significant impact in that respect. One woodchuck can inflict more harm on a vegetable plot than several rabbits.

This is a pestilence far more common than realized, and it offers an excellent opportunity to engage in a new tactic while performing a valuable service to the landowner. However, few hunters are aware of this opportunity, and most farmers think the hunters are interested only in long-range shooting. All it takes to get a crack at these close-in groundhogs is to ask your host if he has such a problem. If so, you can bet on an invitation to be an exterminator!

This is a perfect situation for some cartridges that no longer enjoy high-profile status. The venerable .22 Hornet is one, since it's efficient and is less noisy than some of the hotter loads. Some other good choices are the .17 Rem., .218 Bee, .25/20 Win. and .32/20 Win. Since shots are at close range, this circumstance is also suitable for the .22 Mag and for handguns and archery equipment.

These down-home woodchucks pose a challenge, since they frequently are very wary, having been harassed by dogs and sometimes peppered with shot by the farmer. It takes stealth and patience to score, and if several are present, things get tougher after the first one is bagged.

Something that was mentioned before: woodchucks are just as likely to be found under and around abandoned buildings and under old farm machinery that has been left in the field with vegetation growing up around it.

Sinkholes are places that almost always have woodchuck populations. They're perfect havens, undisturbed by agricultural practices but in proximity to the results. The key to success in hunting these places is to scout them in advance and locate the burrows so the best angle of approach can be determined.

Woodchucks like to have burrows in locations that offer safety and easy access to food sources. Sinkholes are only one of the places that provide both of these advantages. There are several others that are equally attractive.

Fence rows or hedgerows have special appeal, since they are avenues between croplands that provide both cover and travel lanes. Plowing or harvesting can't disturb burrows, yet food sources are literally right at their front doors. In areas where there are rock walls, the same applies.

The way to hunt these sites is to first glass both sides and see if any burrows or animals are visible. If nothing shows, then begin a quiet stalk along the side that you judge to be the most favorable for a stalk. Stop frequently and continue to keep glassing on the area ahead, as well as whatever can be seen on the

One reason farmers dislike woodchucks is that their burrows often cause damage to livestock and farm machinery.

Fence rows can be productive for woodchucks, since they often locate their burrows in the cover that grows up alongside them.

opposite side. Very often, if progress is made quietly enough, it's possible to walk within a few yards of a groundhog sunning itself at the burrow's entrance.

Woodchucks also frequently inhabit small woodlots, but locating the burrows can be difficult, and it's equally hard to hunt them in these places. However, if they're known to be present, by a hunter's sitting at the woods' edge and waiting, there's a chance to get a crack at them as they travel to and from feeding areas.

Free-lancing hunters can find no better way to cover a lot of territory and get in plenty of shooting than by walking railroad tracks, a point of access to hunting territory described earlier in the chapter on squirrels. The embankments along the roadbeds have always been prime places for woodchuck burrows, and like some of the spots just described, they're near or adjacent to agricultural fields. Stalking from the tracks is a quiet approach, and very efficient, since often the hunter is in an elevated position with excellent short- and long-range visibility.

Topographical maps can be useful in checking out local potential for this kind of hunting, because they show the locations where the tracks pass through

A fence post makes a good rest for the scope-sighted Thompson/Center carbine in .17 Remington.

the most farmland. You can select a few sections that look good and make trial runs. Eventually, you'll accumulate a list of those that are the most productive.

One of the benefits of this type of tactic is that it can double your opportunity. For instance, if you walk a couple of miles of track, the return trip provides nearly the same amount of potential. Any animals disturbed will have overcome their caution and again be active.

Walking along railroad tracks is a good way to hunt woodchucks, since they often have dens along the adjacent embankments.

Many railroads have ceased to operate, but their tracks or roadbeds are still intact, so these "avenues" remain available to varmint hunters. After all, traffic on them is of no consequence.

Probably the least-utilized woodchuck hunting method is floating streams and rivers, but it's well worth giving consideration. This is a totally silent and effortless way to stalk, and it gives access to some extremely productive habitat areas. The streamside tree lines serve not only as buffers between cultivated fields but also as ideal places for groundhogs to settle in. A particular advantage is that green vegetation can be found near water the year around in most places, providing food for the animals at times when other foods aren't readily available

Canoes or kayaks have traditionally been the most popular means of conveyance, but in recent years some very sophisticated float-tube designs have been produced. One of the advantages floating offers is access to territory normally not invaded by varmint hunters.

Floating is one of the few methods of woodchuck hunting where shotguns are sometime used. Canoes, kayaks and float tubes are relatively unstable shooting platforms, which often preclude accurate rifle marksmanship. Shotguns with large-size buckshot get good results at distances up to 50 yards, and the pattern size eliminates the necessity of pinpoint accuracy.

One of the most interesting and challenging places to hunt woodchucks is in mountainous regions like the southern Appalachians. There are vastly more animals in the highlands than might be imagined, yet pursuing them

Hunting mountain woodchucks is productive, but it can be tough going at times.

requires considerably different techniques and a lot more physical stamina than most other forms of the sport. Conversely, it can bring out the best in both hunter and quarry.

With few, if any, agricultural crops upon which to depend for subsistence, the high country 'chucks do more diversified foraging than their lowland cousins. Because of this, their feeding patterns are less predictable. Burrow openings are what mountain hunters look for.

The best friend a varmint hunter can have in getting into good mountain groundhog range is a four-wheel-drive vehicle, because much of it is at places where walking in is the only alternative. Even then, some additional foot travel is usually necessary.

The first rule in identifying the spots with the best promise is to determine which hillsides face east. Groundhogs prefer locations that receive morning sunlight, and in the mountains the western slopes remain in shade until the sun is high in the sky. Early light permits groundhogs to begin foraging while it's still cool, and once this is completed, they can spend time sunning at the entrances to their dens.

The highlands afford the opportunity for both long- and short-range shooting. It's sometimes possible to set up on top of a ridge and shoot at woodchucks on the sides of adjacent hills. This kind of setting is one preferred by a clan of Pennsylvania varmint hunters who specialize in the ultimate in extended range shooting. These individuals use custom rifles chambered for .50 caliber cartridges necked down to smaller calibers, even as far as saboted .17 Remington, and military-type range-finding equipment. With the heavier bullets, shots as distant as 1,000 yards can be made, but the lighter ones such as the .17 Remington can't hold up at extremely long ranges. This style of varminting isn't likely ever to enjoy great popularity, but it does indicate that there are always people exploring the outer limits of the sport.

A more strenuous approach to the high country woodchucks is tackling the ups and downs of the terrain on foot and seeking out the animals. In practically every case, the animals will be either above or below your line of travel, and bagging them is more like sniping than anything else. It's also tricky, because as every rifleman knows, steep angle shots increase the chances of a miss. This danger is magnified even more when shooting is done offhand: you're walking along, spot a groundhog and have to fire before it dives into its hole.

Mountain groundhogs' dens on hillsides give them an advantage when hunters approach from a lower level. They have an excellent view of all below, and this is where their attention is usually focused. The odds change when the positions are reversed and the hunter is on top looking down, which is a sound reason for walking the along crests of hills rather than in the valleys.

Hunting from vehicles is popular, and it's a very effective way to bag woodchucks. This gives the hunter great mobility and a stable shooting platform. Driving to the edge of a large field or pasture in a pickup truck and setting up the spotting scope, sandbags and other accessories on the roof provides a close approximation of bench rest shooting. Shooters who use cars equip them with window mounts for both spotting scopes and rifles and get a similar effect. Shooting off the hoods is widely practiced, too.

The laws on the use of vehicles for varmint hunting vary considerably from state to state. Some forbid it entirely, while others permit it on some types of road. There are also locations where it's legal when the vehicle is being used on private land and away from public roads. And it's worth mentioning that in some instances there's a distinction made between firing out the windows and using the vehicle as a shooting platform from the outside.

The top of a pickup truck makes an ideal shooting platform, and provides extra elevation.

There are other advantages to using a vehicle besides convenience. Woodchucks are accustomed to seeing farm machinery, so approaching or entering a field in a car or truck isn't likely to cause the animals any concern. To the contrary, it often allows hunters to get much closer than would otherwise be possible. A second plus applies particularly to pickup trucks, which provide elevation and enable the shooter to see animals that wouldn't be visible from ground level due to cover or undulations in the terrain.

Aside from cars and trucks, there's good utility for the four-wheel all-terrain vehicles that are popular for many other kinds of hunting. Because of their versatility, they give varmint hunters extended range beyond that of conventional vehicles. Equipped with racks for holding guns and storing gear, they are much like magic carpets on which to cover country that would ordinarily have to be traveled on foot.

EQUIPMENT AND ACCESSORIES

Obviously, the right weapon is the most vital equipment item, and any of the varmint rifles discussed in the preceding chapter are suitable. Handguns are becoming increasingly popular with woodchuck hunters, for both short-range and long-range shooting. The Remington XP-100 and Thompson/Center Contender are favorites, and both are available in a wide variety of varmint cartridges. Equipped with a good scope and in the hands of an experienced shooter, each is very accurate at ranges up to 200 yards. When woodchucks can be stalked and approached to within 50 yards or fewer, using big bore pistols with open sights offers handgunners a special challenge. It's a good way to get in some practice that's more fun than on a standard range.

Speaking of the big boomers, woodchucks also offer hunters an ideal situation in which to shoot large-caliber rifles that are normally intended for use on game as large as elephants; cartridges such as the .375 H&H Magnum, .340 Weatherby Magnum, .416 Rigby, .458 Winchester Magnum, and .470 Nitro Express. Woodchucks provide a much smaller target, and accuracy with these big rifles can be improved significantly by shooting in the field rather than on the range. Too, it's a chance to have some fun using rifles that spend most of the time locked up in a gun cabinet.

Next in importance is having the right kind of optics. The ability to locate game, get a precise look at it, and then place bullets accurately at distant

Lots of woodchuck hunters like to go after them with handguns, and no holds are barred in regard to caliber. Shown above, starting from bottom left; Iver Johnson .22 automatic; Thompson/Center Contender with JDJ Special .45–70 barrel, Simmons scope and Harris bipod; Remington XP-100 Varminter in .223 with Leupold scope; Ruger Red Hawk in .44 magnum; Ruger Black Hawk Single Six in .357 magnum.

targets is dependent upon binoculars and rifle and spotting scopes. Without these, the sport of varmint hunting would be restricted to short range shooting with iron sights.

A good rifle scope stands as the top priority, the power range depending on the distance at which one intended to shoot. A 4X scope is quite suitable for reasonably close-range situations, while the 200-yard-plus targets require much higher magnification to achieve precise bullet placement. A hunter can choose from fixed or variable power models with power ranges up to 24X. Due to a highly competitive market, good-quality scope models can be bought at reasonable prices, but the models designed for ultra-long range or target shooting still command a hefty dollar figure.

No hunter should be without a set of good binoculars, because they serve many purposes. Spotting game is one, but they are also very helpful in looking over terrain and developing strategies. Technological advances have made it possible for manufacturers to produce light, compact models of

Taking aim at a woodchuck with the Remington XP-100 from a reclining position.

Woodchucks give hunters the opportunity to use big bore rifles. This custom A-square .416 Rigby packs enough punch to down an elephant.

The Weatherby Alaskan in .340 Weatherby Magnum has a recoil arrester and a good recoil pad, so it's not unpleasant to shoot.

excellent quality that can be carried in a shirt or jacket pocket. However, many hunters prefer larger binoculars with higher magnification and a greater field of view.

Although binoculars are fine for spotting game, spotting scopes with very high magnification make it possible to closely examine the target, determine the best time to shoot and have an instant view of the results. Once used mainly by hunters shooting from fixed positions, several models are now available in sizes and weights very suitable for packing when walking around.

Range finders can be of great help in determining shooting distances, and there while there are several types available, the Bushnell Rangefinder binoculars are the most practical and accurate.

Hunters who don't own one or more Harris bipods are usually those who haven't used one of these devices. The great stability they provide aids immensely in precise bullet placement at long ranges. The bipods attach to the fore end of the rifle and fold away when not in use, and they are equally as good as a sand bag for support. There are several models, including one that extends to permit shooting from a sitting position, an advantage especially valuable when sitting in tall grass.

The Harris bipod extends so a shooter can fire from a sitting position. This is a big advantage when in tall grass.

Since woodchuck hunters get a lot of exposure to the summer elements, using a high-number sunblock, sunglasses and wearing a broad-brimmed hat can help ward off skin and eye problems. Insect repellents are useful items to have along, particularly those that ward off ticks, chiggers, and mosquitoes. Lying on the ground or walking through grass and other vegetation almost always results in encounters with some of these pests.

Another item that's highly practical is a small tarp or ground cloth to use in early morning when the dew is still on the grass, or when recent rains have left the earth soggy. Too, accessories can be spread out and organized better on a ground cover.

For hunters who will be moving around, all of these accessories can be easily carried in a day pack, along with lunch, a canteen of water, and a light rain jacket or poncho.

6

PRAIRIE DOGS

Some animals end up with names that are only half right. The Sea Lion is an example, for while it lives in the ocean, it isn't a feline. The "lion" part results from its similar roar.

The same is the case with the Prairie Dog, which indeed inhabits the region the name suggests, but it isn't a canine. It does "bark," if that's how one chooses to interpret the sound it makes.

Two early French explorers, Louis and Francois Verendrye, who were roaming what is now Canada in the mid-1700s, swung southward into the region that was later to become North and South Dakota and Montana. In the process, they came upon huge colonies of small ground-dwelling animals that sat up, picket-like, on their den mounds and vocally protested the explorers' presence with high-pitched yips. The Verendryes promptly labeled the animal *petit chien*, which means "little dog."

That took care of half of the name. Meriwether Lewis added the "prairie" prefix in 1804. Leading the Lewis and Clark expedition through this

Prairie Dog

same region, he noticed that the little animals were found mostly in the prairies. Apparently he was aware of the title given them by the earlier explorers and chose not to alter the "dog" part. Scientific accuracy in classifying new animals wasn't closely observed in those days, which is why we have several other misnamed species, examples of which are elk, antelope, and buffalo.

The prairie dog is another member of the squirrel family, and certainly the darling of varmint hunters in the areas it inhabits. No other animal is as numerous or as prolific, so there's never any problem finding action in prairie dog country when weather and seasonal conditions are right. In effect, it's the western version of the woodchuck—and then some!

There are four species, Black-tailed Prairie Dog, White-tailed Prairie Dog, Gunnison's Prairie Dog, and Utah Prairie Dog, but the first two are the ones that attract almost all of the varmint hunters' attention. The Gunnison's occupies a much smaller range and is less numerous, and the Utah is classed as endangered.

The White-tailed Prairie Dog is the species with the widest distribution. Before the Great Plains was settled, its range extended from Saskatchewan to the Rio Grande. Within this territory were gigantic dog towns, and there are some early accounts of their size that are truly amazing. One of these, written in 1852 by R.B. Marcy, told of a one-million-acre tract that had an estimated five million inhabitants. At about the same time, John R. Bartlett reported that

The Thompson/Center Carbine has interchangeable barrels, so a prairie dog hunter can use a number of different cartridges by having several extra barrels. It's also easy to switch barrels if one becomes overheated.

he had ridden on horseback for three days along a tributary of the Colorado River in Texas without getting outside the limits of one mammoth and continuous prairie dog community.

Later descriptions of prairie dog populations in particular areas include one by a biologist, Hart Merriam, who in 1900 spent several weeks studying a town near San Angelo, Texas, that was 250 miles long and 100 miles wide. His conclusion was that there were at least four million animals inhabiting it. In 1931, Vernon Bailey claimed that 6,400,000 was a conservative estimate of the prairie dog population of Grant County, New Mexico. And even as late as 1945, Bert Popowski said he saw a dog town in northern Nebraska that paralleled a railroad track for 20 miles.

Today, the majority of large prairie dog villages are on protected lands, and both their range and numbers have been much reduced from pioneer times. Presently, the black-tailed is found from eastern Montana and southwest North Dakota to northwest Texas, New Mexico, and a small part of southeastern Arizona. The white-tailed is a resident of a much smaller pocket of territory that includes southeastern Utah, southwestern Colorado, northeast Arizona, and northwest New Mexico.

What caused the dramatic reduction in the overall prairie dog numbers were the settlement of the Great Plains and the subsequent agricultural development of the land. It was the impression of farmers and ranchers that prairie dogs were in conflict with their interests, so mass extermination projects were initiated. Poison was the main instrument of destruction, because a spoonful of grain soaked with strychnine poured into each burrow opening assured death to all of its inhabitants. Traps were also used, as well as gas, and everyone with a rifle was eager to plink away at them.

The campaigns to wipe out prairie dogs lasted for many years. This factor, along with the reduction of available habitat due to increasing human population and further land development guaranteed that no comeback was possible.

Fortunately, the pressure was gradually reduced, as it became apparent that these animals weren't as detrimental to human efforts as was first believed. They were initially charged with eating grass that ranchers needed to fatten cattle, and while this is true, it isn't their main source of food. Prairie dogs eat many weeds and plants that cattle ignore. There was also the claim that their burrow openings were responsible for breaking the legs of livestock. This may occur to a small extent, but looking at it from a different perspective, the bur-rowing serves to rejuvenate the soil, and abandoned dens are often occupied by various creatures including owls and rabbits, other small rodents, salaman-ders, lizards and snakes.

What has resulted is a sort of live-and-let-live policy between landowners and prairie dogs, as long as the population levels of the dog towns don't be-come excessive. This attitude usually provides an opening and often a warm

Mirage can create problems for long-range rifles such as this.

welcome for varmint hunters, and there's no shortage of opportunities for all-day shoots in the areas where they're still abundant. Given the present circumstances, there's every reason to believe that this sport will continue to be available to shooters throughout the foreseeable future.

Because of its wide range and great numbers, the black-tailed prairie dog is the better known and more sought of the two major species. It is also the larger, weighing from 2 to 3 pounds. The upper body is a pinkish-brown, with off-white underparts. Its tail is slim, sparsely haired and black-tipped, the latter feature which is unique among the species. The ears are small and rounded, and the eyes black. The favored habitat is short-grass prairies.

Prairie dogs are primarily herbivorous, and their diet consists almost entirely of green plants, most of which are the kinds of grasses that are available in any particular area. They favor bluegrass, brome grass, gramagrass, burro grass and purple needle grass, but they will also vary this with grasshoppers and other insects. There is seldom any kind of vegetation in the vicinity of their burrows. They eat this first, but also by eliminating it there is no way predators can approach without being seen.

On hot summer days, prairie dogs feed in the early morning and late afternoon and sleep during the midday heat. In cooler weather, the animals may be active all through the day, although they won't remain above ground during storms. Black-tails seldom venture very far from their burrows, since they are vulnerable once distant from these havens.

The burrows display an instinctive sense of engineering. Conical, well-tamped-down mounds at the entrance serve several purposes, one of which is to create a wall that prevents the burrow from being flooded during rainy weather. The top of the mound provides an elevated observation post, and by varying the height of the mound, the flow of air through the burrow can be regulated.

There are two or more burrow openings, between which is a horizontal tunnel that may be as deep as 14 feet below the surface with several chambers lined with grass that serve as nurseries and another for excrement. Like cats, prairie dogs cover their scat, and when a chamber is filled, it is sealed and another one excavated. Some food may be stored, but generally the animals depend on stored fat to tide them over during the winter. They do not hibernate, but during periods of severe cold or snowstorms they enter a lethargic state and sleep for a few days.

A heavy sand bag on a portable shooting bench makes an extremely solid rest for the shooter.

If a predator such as a snake enters one of the tunnels, it is quickly sealed off, sometimes at both ends, which buries the intruder alive.

Just below the vertical shaft leading to the den's entrance is a short lateral tunnel that provides an out-of-sight listening post, and also a convenient place to turn around without descending into the main tunnel. Quite often, adjoining family groups have interlinking tunnels between the burrows.

Black-tails breed once a year, usually in February and March, and about a month later, have a litter of four or five deaf, blind and hairless young. The offspring emerge into the daylight at about 6 weeks of age, and then depart at about 10 weeks. Full growth is achieved at 6 months. The average life span is from 7 to 8 years.

Prairie dogs cooperate when building a town, but once this is accomplished, it is divided into several wards or neighborhoods. The occupants are friendly to one another, but moving from one neighborhood into another isn't tolerated. One characteristic prevalent among the black-tails is the habit of "kissing." Two animals approach each other and touch noses, then turn their heads to the side and touch incisors. The purpose is for identification among ward and family members that work together building burrows. These same ward members groom each other.

In a dog town there are always sentinels on the alert, and when any sort of danger threatens, one or more will give a sharp bark and hundreds of animals will simultaneously repeat the warning signal and dive into their burrows. Eventually, a few will cautiously peek out to check out the situation, and if no threat is apparent. The all-clear signal consists of what observers call the "yip-jump" display. The prairie dog leaps into the air while emitting a whistling yip, which is then repeated by others in the vicinity. The alarm cry and the all-clear sound are only two of nine distinctive calls that have been identified.

The black-tail has many predators, principal among which are badgers and foxes. Paradoxically, the extermination campaigns that wiped out 90 percent of the prairie dog population also decimated the numbers of what was then their chief predator, the black-footed ferret.

Other enemies are coyotes, bobcats, hawks, owls, eagles, snakes, and, of course, humans. Modern techniques of modifying and improving habitat conditions, plus the effect of all of the predators, combine to maintain a balanced population. This has reduced the desire or need on the part of ranchers to eliminate them.

The white-tailed prairie dog is slightly smaller than its cousin, with upperparts that are a pinkish-buff mixed with black which become slightly lighter on the underparts. The tail is short and white-tipped. The ears are small and rounded, and there are distinctive dark patches above and below the eyes. The nose has a yellowish hue.

One of the major differences between the white-tails and black-tails is the kind of territory they inhabit. Instead of favoring the plains and prairies, the white-tail is oriented to the high country. It occupies mountain regions to altitudes as high as 12,000 feet, and conditions are quite dissimilar from those in the lowlands.

Also, they form smaller colonies and have a lower-key social situation than what is found in the big prairie villages. Fewer burrows are interlinked, and "kissing" and mutual grooming isn't as prevalent.

White-tail burrows don't always have mounds. Often, excavated dirt is simply tossed to the side, and if it is built up slightly, it's seldom tamped down and will wash away during a hard rain. Probably this lack of attention to the mound is because white-tails don't require the kind of visual area needed by the black-tail. For this same reason, they don't clear the vegetation in the vicinity of the den opening.

The mountaineers prefer much the same foods as the black-tails—grasses and a variety of other green plants—but their habitat may restrict their diet to mostly saltbush. Regardless of food choices, all prairie dogs gain weight rapidly during the summer months. A one-pound dog may be twice as heavy by the time fall arrives. In the case of the white-tails, this extra fat must carry them through the entire winter, since unlike the black-tails, they hibernate during the cold months. Usually, they go into this state by September, but some of the younger animals that haven't had this experience may remain active until October, trying to consume a full measure of "winter fuel."

Due to the difference in weather conditions, white-tails breed later than black-tails, usually in the latter part of March when temperatures at the higher elevations moderate sufficiently to make them active. The litters average five, and the young don't appear above ground until May or June. White-tails have a life expectancy of only four or five years.

The principal enemies of the white-tail are birds of prey, bobcats, badgers, and coyotes, and there is a widespread, although unsubstantiated, belief that rattlesnakes take a great toll. Fire and floods kill a fairly large number each year. Man has greatly reduced the population of these animals by the use of poison, gas, and traps. Much of this animosity against them has been significantly reduced, but high-country ranchers still welcome varmint hunters to keep their numbers at an acceptable level.

While it is unfortunate in some respects that the name "dog" was attached to this ground squirrel, the Native Americans regarded them as a diet staple, and it didn't take long for the early settlers to discover that the meat of these animals is quite palatable. There's no doubt that the prairie dog was more than once responsible for saving people from starvation, but more than that, it was a very acceptable source of protein on a regular basis. Apparently, few if any of today's hunters have developed an appetite for them, but it's quite possible that some of the more curious and adventuresome individuals have given them a try. However, it's certain that this doesn't stand a chance of being widely accepted as desirable food, since, theoretically, even if a taste test were to give prairie dog meat good marks, the name association would be instant death to the notion.

One serious problem that affects prairie dog towns is the occasional incidence of bubonic plague epidemics. The organism responsible for this deadly
disease is transmitted by flea bites, and like almost all ground-dwelling members of the rodent order, prairie dogs are commonly victims of flea infestations.
Public health officials monitor the dog towns for this hazard, and when it
shows up, the sites are poisoned and flagged to alert hunters or others who
might approach.

Oddly, this hasn't been a problem of any consequence in the woodchuck population, but this may be because these animals aren't colonial and
closely congregated by nature. No doubt they are susceptible, as any of the
other rodents could be, but prairie dogs are the only ones that have demon-
strated a propensity for such outbreaks.

There may be other problems lurking, though. As recently as 1992, the
deaths of a number of Navajo Indians from a virus strain linked with the excre-
tions of certain rodents have initiated investigations into the possibilities of danger that could be posed by a number of species that inhabit the same region.

This poses a dilemma, because although the prairie dog isn't on the endangered list, some of the other rodents are. This will undoubtedly ignite
more divisive people-versus-protected-species battles that have become commonplace in recent years.

HUNTING METHODS AND ACCESSORIES

All things considered, prairie dog hunting has no peer when it comes to
supplying fast action and plenty of targets to shoot at. Even crow hunting can't
compare, since in situations where an unlimited number of animals are present, an individual may fire as many as 1,000 rounds in a day. What's more, it
can be repeated the next day and for as long as the ammunition holds out.

For those who haven't hunted prairie dogs, a first look at the sport can
make it appear to be a utopian situation. Unlike some other varmint shooting
experiences in which stealth, patience, and various means of subterfuge are required for success, prairie dogs are sitting out in the wide-open spaces by the
thousands, just waiting for hunters to come out and knock them off. All you
have to do is load up and begin cracking away.

All of this is true, but the hitch is that it isn't the whole story. What a cur-
sory observation doesn't reveal are the elements that cause some shooters to

Good binoculars and a quality rifle scope are an ideal combination for prairie dog hunting.

consider it the most challenging, demanding and maddening of all varmint hunting sports. It takes firsthand experience to thoroughly learn what these things are, but a little further thought on the nature of prairie dog territory will help to illuminate some these.

For one thing, much of the range these animals occupy is flat, semi-arid country that is hot and windy during the times when they are most active. The implications of both characteristics are significant, and each has a great deal to do with making prairie dog hunting such a challenge.

To begin with, let's look at hot. That it can be physically uncomfortable is of some consequence, but how it affects shooting is the most important consideration. By far the greatest number of those who seek these rodents are rifle shooters who want to take them at long range, and at this point heat becomes a major player.

Three particular influences stand out as most important:

First, mirage, the shimmering heat waves that rise off the surface of the ground, makes a distant target wiggle like a hula dancer. It's a bugaboo to accuracy that can cause shooters to experience fits of frustration. Nothing can be done about it, and the only way it can be avoided is by limiting activity to the very early hours of the day. And that destroys the chance of doing a lot of shooting.

Second, high-velocity cartridges cause barrels to become hot very rapidly, and the addition of environmental heat creates a situation in which it must be allowed to cool between shots in order to avoid serious damage. If only one rifle is used, the action will necessarily be intermittent. For this reason, veteran 'dog hunters take several rifles along so they can switch around and keep on shooting. The favorite prairie dog rifle among many hunters who don't attempt ultra-long range shooting is the .222 Remington, because it doesn't heat up quickly and can be used for longer periods of time than the high-intensity cartridges. Also, if there's the opportunity to take some animals at closer ranges, some of the less potent, short-range .22s, both rimfire and center-fire, are useful to include in the arsenal.

Third, since most prairie dog hunters handload their ammunition and beef it up to their individual specifications, the rounds must be worked up at temperatures similar to those expected in the field. Heat causes changes in pressure levels, and this factor must be taken into account in order to obtain precision performance. Factory loads aren't critical in this sense, so normal precautions of keeping ammunition out of direct sunlight is all that's required.

Wind is the other factor, and it seems as though it blows more constantly in prairie dog country than anywhere else in America. A calm day is a rarity, which often bewilders varmint hunters as much as if they had suddenly been thrust into a strange world.

It is a paradox, too, because to the shooter, this force is at once both friend and enemy. Wind is the quixotic imp that causes bullets to go astray and the harsh taskmaster that makes learning its vagaries necessary to achieve a high degree of accuracy. "Reading the wind" is a skill that every hunter who shoots at long range yearns to perfect. In the case of prairie dog shooting where light bullets are used, the effects of air movement are more pronounced than on heavier slugs.

There are numerous ways to get a general idea of wind direction and velocity. Tossing up bits of grass or a handful of dust is one, and looking at heat waves through binoculars or a rifle scope to see in which direction they're leaning and how severe the angle is another. Hanging a cotton ball on a string works as an indicator, too, and there's a manufactured device available for a few dollars that measures wind velocity.

Veteran shooters rely primarily on experience and their own judgment to evaluate this factor, and one thing that can be relied upon is to take a shot aimed dead-on at the target and see where the bullet strikes. This will provide a pretty close indication of what's happening between the hunter and whatever he's shooting at unless the wind is gusting. In this case, there simply isn't any way to assure accuracy.

Setting up for a prairie dog shoot near a 'dog town has many of the trappings of a tailgate party, because almost all of the conveniences of home can be brought along. The vehicle is driven to the spot where the shooting will be done, and all of the gear and accessories are unloaded and put into position. This usually includes a bench rest, sandbags, a spotting scope, binoculars, rangefinder, several rifles, a cleaning kit, and plenty of ammunition. In the vehicle, which often is a van, there are refreshments, food, and best of all, shade and sometimes air conditioning. Conducted in this manner, it isn't a sport that creates hardships

Of course, all hunters don't enjoy this kind of comfort, especially those who choose to walk around and take random shots at the animals at whatever distances they may happen to appear. This doesn't require the kind of cartridges used by long range shooters; instead, the .22 WRF Magnum, .22 Hornet, .218 Bee and .25–20 Winchester all are very practical choices and fun to shoot offhand. Prairie dogs, like woodchucks, are hunted with everything from .22 long rifle cartridges to those used for the world's biggest game, but the majority of hunters favor the center-fire .22 and 6mm calibers.

Handgunners find the prairie dog villages excellent places to conduct what is called the "point-and-shoot" system. This is basically instinct shooting

A 22-250 topped with a 6x20X scope is a perfect choice for hunting prairie dogs.

where the gunner carries the weapon casually and fires the instant a prairie dog head pops up without taking time to aim. Practice is needed to hone this skill to a fine edge, and 'dog towns supply the handgunner with plenty of opportunity.

Youngsters living in prairie dog country usually get their first shooting opportunity plinking away at these animals, once they have been indoctrinated into firearms use and safety rules. Prairie dogs are excellent targets for their initial trips afield. They guarantee plenty of action, and also provide practical experience in judging range and learning the basics of bullet performance.

Eastern varmint hunters who want a chance to make a prairie dog expedition now have plenty of assistance available, because there are at least four states in which there are outfitters who specialize in these animals. Most have, or can arrange, accommodations, meals, licenses, and guides. The best reference to these services is *The Varmint Hunter*, the official publication of The Varmint Hunters Association, Inc.

Some of the outfitters feature animals other than prairie dogs (some in the game category), so such ventures can be truly classed as an "American safari", on which several species can be collected in a single trip. It's also a lot less costly!

EQUIPMENT AND ACCESSORIES

Rifles have been discussed, but it's important to mention optics. The ranges involved and the conditions that exist make quality optics a necessity. Variable rifle scopes and spotting scopes are the best, since they can be manipulated to help reduce mirage. Also, a good range finder will be very useful in estimating distance—an extremely difficult feat in flat country with so small an animal as a target.

Since prairie dogs are ordinarily shot from fixed positions and at long ranges, having steady shooting platforms is essential. There are some very well-designed benches that fold down compactly and take up little room in a vehicle but can be erected in minutes. One- and two-man benches are available.

Good rests are essential. Shooting bags filled with sand or shot are probably the most commonly used, but there are several mechanical rifle rests available, some of which have adjustments for fine-tuning the rifle's position. Bipods are useful on and off the bench, and there are models for both rifles and handguns. Shooter's tripods are also available.

Since intense heat, bright sunlight and wind are to be expected in prairie dog country, shooters should anticipate this by taking along light, loose clothing, preferably with long-sleeved shirts and a broad-brimmed hat; sun screen; good shooting glasses; lip balm; and plenty of liquids.

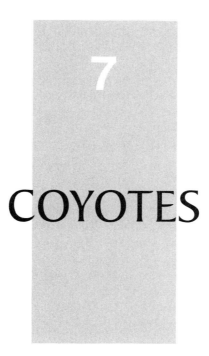

COYOTES

The coyote belongs to the same family as the domestic dog, but except for similarities in appearance with some species such as the German shepherd, the resemblance ends there. To many, this animal is better characterized as one of man's worst enemies, and it's unquestionably one of the most persistent. Indian legend has it that the coyote will be the last animal on earth before the world ends, and there is ample evidence to support this belief. No animal in North America possesses greater survival skills, and it's doubtful that any others can match wits with the coyote. The Navajo Indians refer to the coyote as "God's dog," and rank its intelligence well above that of the wolf.

Also, contrary to popular myth that depicts the fox as the most sly and cunning of the wild animals, the comment of an expert in predator control defies this. He says, "The dumbest coyote with half its brains knocked out has more sense than the smartest fox."

Other members of the Canidae clan are the wolves and foxes, but the coyote, *Canis latrans*, has proved to be the most adaptable and versatile of

Coyote

them all. According to location, the color of the coat may vary considerably, but in general the upper parts are a grizzled gray, sometimes interspersed with brown or reddish tints, with buff undersides. The legs, feet and ears are yellow-ish to rusty, and the tail is bushy with a black tip. When the coyote is running, the tail droops. Its general appearance is dog-like, with prominent ears and a long, narrow muzzle. The coyote is extremely fast and agile and can move at speeds up to 40 mph, fast enough to roll a jack rabbit, but it usually cruises along at 25–30 mph. Weights are generally in the 20– to 50–pound range. It can also make leaps of up to 14 feet.

Coyotes communicate with a variety of vocal sounds that consist of barks, yelps, howls, and yaps that are ordinarily heard at dusk, dawn or in the night. The calls help keep members of the pack alert to their location and re-unite them when separated. Often one call will initiate a chorus of howling re-sponses, resulting in the kind of eerie serenade that was frequently heard in old western movies while the cowboys were gathered around the campfire. Barking alone usually signals a defensive attitude at the den or in guarding a kill. Although coyotes hunt at night, they are equally active during daylight hours, particularly when hunting rodents and other creatures that aren't moving about in darkness.

There is no particular habitat that can be described as typical, since these animals can accommodate practically any kind of environmental situation. In the West, coyotes are most commonly associated with open plains, while in the East, brushy areas are usually preferred. As population levels increase and more coyotes are in proximity to populated areas, they are at home wherever they may be.

Coyotes mate for life, or at least for long periods, and travel as a pair during most of the year. They do not normally live in dens, but they select one as a nursery site before the pups are born. Dens may be in abandoned badger, fox or woodchuck burrows; in caves, hollow logs or culverts; or the female may dig into the soft earth of stream or riverbanks to create her own birthing chamber. Breeding takes place during February to April, with litters averaging six pups born in April to June. During this period and until the pups are weaned and out on their own, the male and female are constant companions, with the male sharing the duties of parenthood. This is the time when adult animals are the most vulnerable, since much more food must be gathered to feed the young. This increases activity and causes coyotes to be bolder and more aggressive.

Once the young are weaned and mobile, usually by late summer, the den is abandoned and the family travels together while the adults teach the pups how to obtain food. Small rodents, young birds, farm crops, and road kills are typical beginners' fare. By late fall the young are on their own, living solitary lives and establishing their own territories.

The phenomenon of coy-dog, crosses between coyotes and domestic dogs, is much discussed among laymen, but this happens rarely and only under certain circumstances. Instances of this hybridization occur when coyotes move into a new area in which there often aren't enough of their own kind around. When the mating urge becomes strong in January and February and another coyote can't be found, a dog may be selected as a substitute. That's the only reason it happens, because coyotes prefer to breed with their own kind. Once enough coyotes are present, the dog reverts to the position of being just another part of their diet.

Coyote/wolf crosses have been documented, but coyote/fox interbreeding doesn't occur. Coyotes hate foxes and will kill adults and raid dens

This big male coyote was called in and killed in the woods as it foraged for rodents.

to destroy and eat young pups. When coyote density increases in an area also inhabited by foxes, the population of the latter species invariably declines. It's a result of the well-known "peck order" in which the bigger and stronger species has the upper hand—or paw. This same situation occurs in places where wolf and coyote populations overlap, in which case the coyote is the loser.

Coyotes stake out individual territories with urine or feces, but they are always loosely associated and communicating with others in the vicinity. These come together as packs which at times travel and hunt together, allowing them to take on larger prey than a single animal could handle. This is a habit shared with their cousins, the wolves, and both species have some very sophisticated strategies much like military operations that involve luring, ambushing and swarming maneuvers.

Where food is concerned, there is almost no limit to what the omnivorous coyote can and will ingest. Rabbits, mice, gophers, ground squirrels, rats, and voles are staple items. Included also are badgers, bobcats, peccaries, woodchucks, marmots, skunks, weasels, pheasants, quail, and ducks. On up the scale, they readily take the young of deer, elk, and antelope, and also the adult animals when they can bring them down. On the domestic side, they are serious predators of sheep, pigs, poultry, and cattle. They also eagerly devour dogs and house cats.

That's not all. They are fond of all kinds of fruits and berries, grasshoppers and other insects, birds, frogs, salamanders, snakes, toads, corn, watermelons, and cantaloupe. When times are tough they will eat carrion and cattle dung. Worst of all, they have been known to kill small children and attack adults.

The coyote's diet in the West isn't as diversified as in the East, where broader food choices can be found. A study conducted in Tennessee for several years by Memphis State University provides an idea of what they ingest in their southeastern range: 42.4 percent of the coyote stomachs contained rodent remains; 27.9 percent, rabbit; 24.3 percent, deer; 20.2 percent, livestock; 13.5 percent, insects; 11.9 percent, nongame birds; 2.2 percent, reptiles and amphibians; 1.1 percent, shrews; 0.4 percent, opossum; 31.5 percent, persimmon; 21 percent, other vegetation; 16 percent, grass; 8 percent, miscellaneous.

Except for man, the coyote is practically free from natural enemies throughout most of its range now that the bear and mountain lion numbers have diminished. However, these creatures never posed more than a token threat, even when their populations were high.

The history of the coyote in North America is one of constant range expansion. These animals were first documented in the United States more than 200 years ago along the Arizona-Mexican border. From this base, the animals began spreading northward through the western states, into Canada and Alaska. Next, they moved eastward through the Canadian provinces, the Midwest, and on to the Northeast. The Southeast was the last region to be invaded, with the first animals appearing in the 1970s. Apparently the Mississippi River was for a long time a barrier to their usual west-to-east migrations. Today the coyote's range extends from Central America to Alaska and east to the Atlantic Ocean. Its common name was derived from the Nahuatl Indian word, *coyotl*, which means, "barking dog." In the Southwest, coyote is usually pronounced ki-o'-tee, but in the northern and eastern part of its range, ki'-oat is more common. Cowboys often referred to them as "prairie warblers" or "ki-dogs."

The magnitude of this predator's impact wasn't realized until ranchers arrived in the Southwest, but the revelation wasn't long in coming. Once livestock, particularly cattle and sheep, were present, the slaughter began. Calves and ewes were killed by the thousands, and maintaining herd populations in the face of the onslaught was often difficult. It was at this point that the coyote became the number one enemy of ranchers, and a war of eventually enormous proportions was initiated against them with its goal to eradicate the species.

It was a no-holds-barred effort in which every means conceivable was utilized. Shooting couldn't make a sufficient dent in their numbers, so traps, explosives, gas, poison, and snares were added to the tools of combat. Later, aerial hunting was added. Bounties were offered, and the government also joined forces with the ranchers. How many animals were killed during the early years isn't known, but through the efforts of the Department of Agriculture's Animal Damage Control Program more than three and one-half million coyotes were eliminated between 1937 and 1981. This doesn't count animals destroyed by other agencies and individuals. Today, the cooperative predator control program destroys from 65,000 to 85,000 coyotes annually at a cost of $11 million in funds made available by various state, federal, county, and private sources.

As in the past, the eradication programs are carried out most aggressively in the western states, since this is where the greatest economic impact occurs. The problem is that advanced techniques haven't helped much, and Compound

1080, the most effective poison ever developed for use against the coyotes, continues to be banned by the federal government. Stockmen rail against the prohibition, because they claim that this is the only weapon that can save them from economic ruin, while opponents maintain that even Compound 1080 won't stop the coyote depredation and could endanger other species of wildlife.

All told, the effects of the reduction projects have been quite the opposite of what was intended. Instead of diminishing the species, coyotes have become even more numerous despite these efforts, and their range has continued to expand. Though once primarily associated with wild places, coyotes now frequent populated areas, foraging in city neighborhoods, robbing garbage cans and eating whatever else they can find, including domestic pets. In Los Angeles, which has one of the largest coyote populations of any major U.S. city, one study showed that 80 percent of their diet was dogs and cats.

What has maintained and increased coyote numbers is their amazing reproductive capabilities. Under pressure, litter sizes increase, and when it is removed, fewer pups are born. Biologists call this a "density dependent" reproductive mechanism, similar to that which operates in rabbits. Evidence from studies shows that in Yellowstone National Park (where coyotes are protected) litter sizes average one to two, but in places where they are heavily hunted and pursued the litter size may be 16 or more. An added element is that when these conditions exist, the animals are not only more fertile but also breed at younger ages.

The coyote problems in the West have been vexing enough, but the animal has become even more controversial in the some of the other regions it occupies. The reason is that in addition to continuing its assault on whatever domestic livestock and farmer's crops that are available, it is having a decided impact on antelope, deer, and turkey populations that has both hunters and biologists concerned. There is evidence that in some areas coyotes are killing up to twice as many deer as hunters, and there is also plenty of proof that turkeys' numbers are also being significantly reduced by this predation.

What happened in Nebraska is a good example of this problem. As more coyotes appeared in the state, the pronghorn antelope populations began to dwindle. It was obvious that coyote predation was the reason, and in a two-year study to reduce fawn mortality, some interesting information was gained regarding control measures. The first year, 1990, by removing 112 coyotes from a 170-square-mile study area, antelope fawn success rose to 62 percent inside the zone compared with 25 percent outside. The following year, 88 coyotes were removed from another 150-square-mile study area in which fawn successes jumped to 58 percent against the outside figure of 35 percent.

The conclusion was obvious: reduce coyote numbers and increased fawn survival rates will help assure stable antelope populations.

Another excellent illustration of this approach is seen in a Texas study involving coyote predation on whitetail deer fawns. The test site was a large ranch divided into two parts. On one half, coyote control measures were carried out, while coyotes occupying the other half were unmolested. The expected occurred: fawn survival rates rose by 500 percent in the section where coyotes were controlled as compared with the other half.

There are many other examples. Biologists in Minnesota believe that whitetail deer fawns comprise up to 70 percent of the coyote's diet in the months when birthing occurs, May through July, and much the same conclusion has been drawn in most other states where studies have been conducted. In the northeastern states of Maine, New Hampshire, Vermont, New York, and Massachusetts, deer populations are being heavily impacted, and a Maine wildlife biologist, Henry Hilton, says that coyotes are killing more than twice as many deer annually as hunters.

Regardless of location, predation isn't limited to fawns. Coyotes kill thousands of adult deer, taking not just the old or weak animals but healthy ones, as well. Yearlings are particularly vulnerable to either individual animals or packs. This has a significant effect of wildlife management programs, even when deer herds are in good shape in terms of numbers, since predation influences the buck/doe ratios biologists seek to establish in order to produce quality animals and maintain a good gene pool. For instance, if half of the fawns destroyed by coyotes are males, it's impossible to achieve the desired results.

So looking at all of the problems the coyote poses for hunters, farmers and game biologists, what are the prospects for finding some kind of solution? According to Gary Cook, a biologist with the Tennessee Wildlife Resources Agency and one of the top coyote experts in the East, they're good if the situation is viewed realistically:

"What's most important in any talk about coyotes is to recognize that this is a survivor that can adapt to any conditions. It's here to stay, and we have to look at how we can coexist with it and not make the same mistakes that have been made in the past by attempting to eradicate it with trapping, poisoning and bounty hunting. We've used everything short of atomic bombs as control measures, and none has succeeded. Proof of this is that there are more coyotes on the North American continent today than any other time in history. The plain truth is that the coyote cannot be eliminated, and it will defeat any efforts we instigate to do so. If we're not intelligent enough by this time to understand this, we'd better give up and start over!

"Probably the best thing that can happen is for hunters to recognize that the coyote is the most intelligent and challenging animal they're ever likely to seek. As such, coyotes are truly trophy animals, as worthy of bragging about as an eight-point buck. It takes a particular type of hunter to get good at killing coyotes, too. You have to work at it, because if you don't, the animal will make a fool of you early in the game.

"What we and other agencies across the country have done is to enlist the aid of hunters, explaining that by learning coyote control techniques they can form mutually beneficial associations with landowners. Coyote control has become a necessary part of farm maintenance, and if a hunter can get good at harvesting them, he can open up land for other kinds of hunting. In the old days, when farmers had predator problems, they called in the hunters, so the coyote offers a chance to revive that tradition.

"These ideas are catching on, and more varmint hunters are finding that hunting coyotes is more exciting and enjoyable than some other forms of the sport, and also more versatile."

Many different kinds of coyote control measures have been devised for landowners. Electric fences are especially useful for tracts of up to about 100 acres, but unlike the common one- or two-strand types, these have seven strands that don't permit getting under or over the charge. Game agencies also supply landowners with information and instructions on how to trap coyotes. This requires special techniques, since coyotes are extremely cautious and instinctively wary of devices intended to end their lives. They learn to spot trap sets. A demonstration of their adroitness is that there have been occasions where coyotes have picked up traps and deposited them elsewhere without setting them off.

"Guard dogs are helpful," says Cook, "especially big animals such as the Pyrenees, a gentle species, but with enough bulk to be intimidating to coyotes who see them in the fields or on farm premises."

Cook says that total elimination of coyotes is a bad idea because:

"First of all, it isn't possible, and second, there's a place for these animals in the overall picture. Coyotes eliminate a great many rodents, and not all are guilty of causing farmers grief.

"The way to view this is to look for the few coyotes in an area that are causing damage. For example, a farmer may have a large tract of land frequented by as many as 100 coyotes and still have no problems, while the farm next door may have one coyote which has developed a taste for poultry, livestock, or maybe the watermelon patch. That's the animal that should be eliminated instead of declaring war on all coyotes in the area. As with people, a couple of bad actors can give a neighborhood a bad name."

Strangely, there are people who like to eulogize carnivores such as grizzly bears, mountain lions, wolves, and coyotes, claiming that they are noble creatures and symbols of nature. They view them as underdogs—man being the ruthless villain threatening their existence.

It is a false premise, particularly in the case of the coyote, since human existence is ultimately more threatened than that of this daring and durable animal. Something else: hunters and trappers recognize and respect the coyotes' intelligence and ability to survive.

The truth is that the coyote is a cold-blooded killer that stalks calves, ewes, and fawns relentlessly. The observer, watching a coyote eagerly gobble down a newborn fawn and walk away, will surely conclude that the coyote is a cunning, vicious marauder. In Disney's classic, *Bambi*, what if the coyote had been the scoundrel that threatened Bambi instead of the hunter? Would emotionalism then be directed at this predator?

Mark Twain had some comments about the coyote, but it's very likely that he didn't know much about the animal and may have written these off the top of his head:

"The coyote is a living, breathing allegory of want . . . always poor, out of luck, and friendless . . . he is so spiritless and cowardly that even while his exposed teeth are pretending a threat, the rest of his face is apologizing for it."

Facts prove quite the opposite, of course, and they should take precedence over emotion. Those who choose to adore the coyote would be well advised to take a look at all the facts.

HUNTING METHODS

The tactics that have been used in sport hunting for coyotes and predator control include going after them on foot or on horseback, in vehicles, and in airplanes and helicopters. In recent years, some of these methods have become illegal in most places, with only government predator control personnel allowed to use them.

Predator calling totally revolutionized the sport of coyote hunting, and it stands as the most important tactic a hunter can employ in killing not only coyotes but also a number of other pest animals.

It isn't a recent development. The late J. Murray Burnham, a Texan, is acknowledged as the father of predator calling. Burnham stumbled upon the idea early in the century when he was a young boy. He observed a jack rabbit tangled in a barbed wire fence, emitting screams of pain. Moments later, three wolves came running in and quickly devoured it. Realizing that the animal's distress calls were what attracted the wolves, Burnham began practicing making the sounds with his mouth, and within a short time had the mimicry perfected.

To test out his new skill, he took a companion along and returned to the same spot where the jack rabbit had met its end. They both had rifles, since the idea of facing a wolf pack had them somewhat nervous. The unexpected happened. Just as they arrived at the scene, they saw seven wolves in pursuit of a doe, which they quickly brought down and began to tear apart. Burnham pulled his companion down behind a log and began calling. The effect was far beyond what he had expected. An old wolf standing guard while the others ate immediately came running straight to the call, and seconds later the others abandoned the dead doe and followed. Both boys started shooting, and by the time the wolves finally dispersed and ran, four of them lay dead.

From that point Burnham's reputation as a predator killer extraordinaire grew, and at one time responding to a plea from a rancher whose land was overrun with foxes, he called in and killed 105 in six hours. He kept reducing them throughout the year and ended with a total of 451.

The technique Burnham developed was the mouth call, which remains as deadly today as when he first used it. It's a simple process but one that requires some practice and experimentation. Here's how it is done:

Begin by getting the inside of your mouth as dry as possible by swallowing several times. Then open your mouth slightly and pull your lips back inside over your teeth and at the same time gently sucking in air, using the air in your mouth as a sort of reverse bellows. Keep at it, varying the pressure on your lips until you begin producing some squeaking sounds. Once this is accomplished, keep practicing until you can get consistent tones. After that, the

Predator calls were invented by J. Murray Burnham, and since that time a great many variations have been produced, as this assortment of mouth-operated models indicates.

sounds can be manipulated by cupping one of your hands over your mouth and moving it back and forth or bringing it closer to mute the call when an animal is extremely close. Eventually, the process feels natural, and creating the sounds is almost effortless.

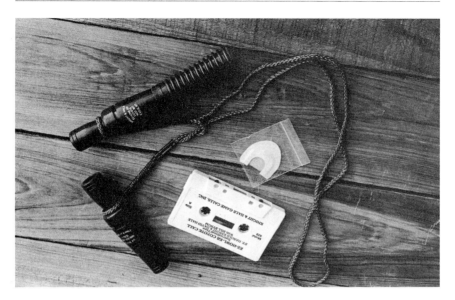

This predator kit comes with three calls and an instructional tape.

Although this technique is still useful, there are now several manufactured calls that reproduce the rabbit distress cries and many other sounds that attract predators. J. Murray Burnham himself invented a number of these, as well as calls designed to lure other animals. His two sons, Murray and Winston, carried on the tradition, forming Burnham Brothers Company and eventually expanding the selection beyond mouth- and hand-operated calls to electronic devices that offer a wide variety of sounds. These have significant advantages, the principal one being that the sounds are generated from tapes or computer chips and are duplications of the actual distress sounds made by various creatures. Among these are rabbit shrieks; mouse squeaks; coyote and fox pup yowls; woodpecker screeches; fawn, calf and ewe bawls; and other signals that something is dying and it's time for the coyote to move in and get its share. Another is that advanced technology allows units that are very light, compact and easily portable. Another prominent predator-call company, Johnny Stewart, even produces a battery-operated device that can be worn on the belt and plays miniature records.

Even with the authenticity of the sounds produced by the electronic calls, hunters who use them almost always also employ conventional calls to

A closer view of some predator calls, including the popular, bulb-type mouse squeaker at extreme left.

obtain maximum results. This permits additional sounds to be mixed in, and both the volume and the tempo of the mouth-operated models can be adjusted according to how the coyote is reacting.

For beginning varmint hunters, the electronic calls provide a special benefit. Listening to the actual bird and animal sounds and trying to duplicate them as closely as possible works a lot better than trying to learn by reading instruction books.

Being successful on a regular basis requires more than just calling. The craftiness and intelligence of the animal has already been described, but something else is worth adding: the coyote possesses eyesight and hearing as keen as that of the wild turkey, along with an equal amount of wariness. What makes it even more elusive and hard to fool is that it also can smell!

With these kinds of capabilities, it's obvious that camouflage is essential, and there's no question that the three-dimensional ghillie suits come as close to providing total invisibility as any other type. This ingenious kind of camou-

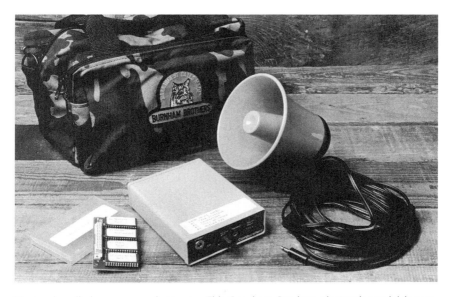

Electronic calls have come a long way. This Burnham Brothers electronic model is computerized and very compact. All of the items fit into a small handbag.

Another popular electronic call is the Johnny Stewart model, which features a wide variety of tapes for hunting many kinds of predators.

A coyote hunter inserts a tape into a Johnny Stewart electronic call.

This short-range, battery-operated, electronic call can be worn on the belt. The tiny records can be changed in seconds.

You can virtually disappear when wearing the Ghillie suit three-dimensional camouflage, which is ideal for coyotes.

flage was invented back in the 1800s by Scottish gamekeepers (called ghillies) to aid them in catching poachers. The Royal Scottish Guards first used ghillie suits during World War I, but they didn't appear on the U.S. hunting scene until the late 1900s. Since that time they have become the standard for serious coyote, fox, and crow hunters because of their superiority over two-dimensional camouflage. Ghillie suits are also especially effective for use in hunting many other kinds of game animals and birds.

There's a difference in hunting in open country and in places such as woods or broken country where visibility is limited. At the former sites, approaching coyotes can often be seen at a distance, permitting the hunter to be better prepared for its arrival. Just as important, its reactions to the call can be gauged. In tighter cover, the coyote may be almost upon the hunter before it is seen.

There are several factors that influence how well a coyote will respond to a call. If very hungry, it's likely to exhibit less caution. Young coyotes that haven't had contact with such situations also tend to be easier to lure in. The placement of the caller is important, too. Some kinds of locations suggest a trap, and the animals will avoid them. Coyotes almost invariably approach prey from downwind, and when in more dense cover, it's necessary to get off a shot before the coyote picks up the human scent.

Hunters in open country often use rifles to pick off the animals well before they're anywhere near, which mainly satisfies their desire to shoot at long distances, but it also prevents having to worry about bringing the coyote into really close range.

Of the favorite coyote cartridges, the .243 Winchester, .25–06 Remington and 6mm Remington stand out as the top three. All have sufficient punch to cleanly kill a coyote, whereas the .222 and .223 Remington are a little light and sometimes don't perform as effectively. Many hunters use larger calibers—.270 Winchester, .30–06 Springfield, 7mm Remington Magnum and even some of the big boomers like the 300 Weatherby Magnum or .375 H&H Magnum—since the 'dogs are excellent target practice for big game.

In the places where night hunting is allowed, the shotgun is often the weapon of choice, because all shots can be made at very close range. Again, it's important to select the proper gauge and shot size. Two of the best choices for this are the Benelli 3 1/2inch 12 gauge pump and automatic shotguns. Nobody can argue with these when using loads of 00 buckshot as

A pair of coyote hunters moves into position in a frost-covered field in early morning.

adequate exterminators, but one should pattern the gun in advance to see how broadly the shot are distributed at the approximate 40-yard distance the coyote is anticipated to be when the trigger is pulled. The goal is to get as many of the big pellets into it as possible, because coyotes often take a lot of killing.

Daytime hunting in heavy cover is also a good place for a shotgun, although some hunters prefer rifles with open sights for the purpose.

Scouting an area before setting up to call and hunt is always wise, and if there are animals in the area, finding signs isn't difficult. Coyotes move around a lot, and their preferred paths are along trails, dirt roads or around the perimeters of open fields or water holes. There will be an abundance of droppings along such routes, and plenty of tracks. Setting up near these lanes increases the chances of producing action. The place you choose should be where you have a good field of view, away from bushes or timber. Coyotes determined to investigate a call will cross open country without hesitation. If it's necessary to set up in the woods, you're likely to have only brief glimpses of the predator, and the chances of not seeing it at all are pretty good.

Probably the most valuable thing a hunter can do to learn a lot about coyotes or other predators is to call them in and observe their actions without the intention of doing any shooting. By doing this, full attention can be devoted to seeing all of an animal's habits and idiosyncrasies. It helps build a storehouse of information that will prove extremely valuable, and which will inevitably make one a much better hunter. The hunter-predator game is always one that is won by the smartest of the adversaries, so a hunter never can know too much about any critter.

This kind of practice calling can have drawbacks, though. If the animal spots the caller or is in some way alarmed, it may become call-shy and be difficult or impossible to lure in again. This is especially true when young animals are being called in during late summer and early fall months, because these are the ones you'll be seriously hunting in the winter and spring. The best solution is to use a different sound when practice calling than the one you employ when actually hunting.

Something to remember is that coyotes will respond to calls as readily at night as in the daytime, so if hunting after dark is allowed where you live, your potential is broadened. Night hunting embodies a few more thrills and excitement because there's so little visibility and things can happen so quickly.

The Mark V Super Predator Master is a fine varmint rifle, available in a wide variety of commercially loaded cartridges.

One of the most practical and deadly additions to the arsenal of tactics that can be used to kill coyotes has been decoys. Calling is a very potent lure, but placing out a replica of something upon which a coyote normally feeds can double the shooter's chances.

There are a number of decoys that can be used, some of which are applicable year around, and others that have great appeal only seasonally. The high degree of predation on fawns has been detailed, so during the months in which the females are giving birth, these newborns are a priority food item for coyotes. It is at this period when an antelope or deer fawn decoy can cause a hungry coyote to lose all caution and come racing in for an easy meal. To watch it is amazing, because the animal's behavior is the opposite of what one would normally expect. Fawn decoys can be easily made by obtaining a form from a taxidermist and using spray paint to create the right color pattern. It doesn't have to be exact: even a general resemblance to a fawn is enough to bring in a coyote. Hunters using this method rack up high scores for as long as the birthing season lasts. After that, fawn decoys have some value, but there are other kinds that are better.

One of these is a rabbit decoy, which can be either a mounted specimen or one of the stuffed animals that can be bought in a toy store. The advantage of the manufactured kind is that some are battery-equipped and display movement, usually in the ears. This is a critical advantage, because coyotes have extremely good vision, and they can spot this from quite far away. The wiggling ears are all the more reason to verify their notion that this is the real thing.

During the period when deer are giving birth, a fawn decoy is incredibly effective in luring coyotes.

Other stuffed animal toys work well, also. Dogs are probably the second choice of most hunters (and again, if they exhibit motion, all the better). Possibly cats and teddy bears would work, too. The main thing is having an object that catches the attention of the coyote while the caller, or callers, are helping to work the animal into a feeding frenzy.

Nothing much has been said about long-range coyote hunting, especially the kind that's conducted without calls, camouflage or decoys. However, it's a form of the sport that attracts a large number of participants. One of the regions where much of this is conducted is the Great Plains where there are plenty of wide-open spaces, but there are also many locations in the eastern U.S. where similar types of terrain can be found.

What these shooters do is situate themselves at a place like a small rise or hill where a lot of territory can be observed, then sit and glass it until a coyote is spotted. It may be that the animal is 300 yards away, or maybe 600 yards, but that's where the challenge lies. This is a breed of rifle hunters who yearn for ultra-long-range opportunities, and their rifles reflect this urge. The .220 Swift and .22–250 Remington are favorites for the super-long shots. Coyotes passing closer may be taken with a .25–06 Remington or .243 Winchester. Because they usually drive right up to the spot where they intend to set up, they can carry along all of the gear and rifles they want.

For these hunters, the action may be somewhat slower than for the callers, but since their main goal is accurate bullet placement, how many coyotes they bag isn't all that important.

Bow hunters get into coyote hunting in a big way, too, since with calls the animals can be brought to within easy range. When they shoot, there's no loud sound, and even if there's a miss, unless the coyote has spotted the hunter's movement, it may not be alarmed, staying in place to give the archer a second try. The twin challenges of calling and the use of primitive equipment are especially satisfying to those who bow-hunt, and the number of bowmen seeking coyotes is increasing significantly.

In the Northeast, where packs of hounds are used to pursue bears and bobcats, hunters have discovered that coyotes make for plenty of sport in the off-season. Coyotes offer challenge, and with the increasing population, there's no shortage of animals to go after. This isn't a new idea. Many years ago some southern foxhunters imported a few coyotes to see if they would provide the same amount of sport as their cousins, but the experiment didn't prove successful. The remnants of this unauthorized stocking became the first coyotes to inhabit the Southeast previous to the major invasion.

One other kind of hunter deserves to be mentioned, even though this person doesn't contribute to the reduction of coyote numbers. This is the individual who hunts with a camera, using the same tactics and techniques, but shooting with a mechanism that does not harm other than to alert the coyote to danger. Their sensitive ears almost always pick up the click of the shutter, and this makes every photo opportunity a one-shot proposition. Actually, there are quite a few gun hunters who carry a camera and switch off occasionally to press a shutter release instead of squeezing a trigger. It's a satisfying alternative.

EQUIPMENT AND ACCESSORIES

Total camouflage is very important when hunting coyotes, so those who plan to seek these animals throughout the year will require a variety of patterns to match seasonal conditions, and they will also need clothing that accommodates different weather conditions. As for concealing the face, some hunters like nets, while others prefer the camouflage grease paint, since this can't get in the way by catching on twigs or branches.

Often there's adequate natural cover available, but if not, there are a number of excellent light, portable blinds on the market that are easy to set up and which work very well. Some are even reasonably weatherproof, which helps under certain conditions.

The right kind of masking scent is very useful in preventing a coyote approaching from downwind from detecting hunters' presence, and skunk odor is particularly effective for this purpose.

Having a number of different calls is very important, since situations differ and sometimes a particular kind of sound is required. Calls shouldn't be selected at random, but rather added once their value in the field has been established. Advice from experienced hunters will help in picking the right ones. This is in reference to hand- or mouth-operated models. Where electronic calls are concerned, it's a matter of what programs you wish to use based on what coyotes prey on in your area, and what time of year it is.

If you plan to hunt at night, there are numerous kinds of lights developed specifically for varmint hunters, including hand-held spotlights and ones that plug into automobile or truck cigarette lighter sockets and generate up to

Where night hunting is permitted, lights such as these will handle all of a hunter's needs. The top four are Coleman hand-held lights, the most powerful of which is the one-million candlepower unit on the left. Below, left to right, are the TopSpot that can be worn as a headlight or folded up and hand-held; the Browning Lightning Bug headlight; and the Browning Micro Ballistic Lite.

one million candlepower. Headlights are very handy, as are the lights that attach to the gun barrel. To avoid spooking animals with lights, the use of a red lens is quite effective. The theory is that this reduces the heat produced by white light, which the eyes of predators can't tolerate. It isn't the illumination that matters, but the kind of illumination.

Extremely important additions to hunting after dark are Bushnell's Night Vision scopes and binoculars. These devices permit hunters to see approaching animals and get ready to shoot well in advance. They also have many other outdoor activities, including camping, backpacking, hiking, fishing, boating, and nature study.

8

THE FOXES

The sly, clever fox is well known to the American public, for it has long been the subject of songs, children's stories, comic books and animated cartoons, usually acting as the villain. In addition, the word fox is commonly used in the language in various ways, some derogatory, some complimentary.

What brought about its "bad guy" reputation is the fondness foxes have for domestic fowl, particularly chickens. They're notorious for midnight raids on henhouses, and they won't pass up the chance to grab a duck, goose or turkey. The economic impact is small, but the level of indignation is high.

Hunters view the fox quite differently, because its cunning and intelligence poses a formidable challenge few other animals can match. Trying to "outfox the fox" is always a tough proposition, regardless of what hunting method is employed. No one who has pursued this cunning canine can help respecting its ability to often elude the best efforts of both men and dogs.

There are four major species of foxes on the North American continent, and their distribution is such that almost no place is without one or more of

Gray fox

them. The ones best known are the Red Fox and Gray Fox, since their ranges are the most extensive. The others are the Swift or Kit Fox and the Arctic Fox. All are members of the *Canidae* family, which also includes the wolves and the coyote.

The red fox, the most abundant of them all, is indigenous to America, although some of the early settlers were apparently unaware of the fact. In the mid-eighteenth century, wealthy landowners in the northeastern states of New York, Maryland, New Jersey, Delaware, and Virginia who enjoyed the English tradition of riding to the hounds were stymied by the gray fox's ability to climb trees. To bring the sport up to par, they imported red foxes from England, only to discover later that there were already native red foxes in the region.

What resulted was that eventually the native and imported stock intermingled and the range kept expanding until virtually the entire continent was populated. Much of the growth came about as a result of land being cleared for farms. This activity provided ideal habitat for the red fox, which likes open areas bounded by woodlands and brushy fence rows that offer protection. The coming of agriculture also brought about a great increase in rabbits and the small rodents that comprise a large part of the fox's diet.

Red fox

Yet with the increase in population came pressure on the red fox other than that applied by hunters and hounds. Their fur became highly popular for women's coats and neckpieces, and the number of trappers seeking these animals increased dramatically. Also, a great hue and cry arose among farmers to eliminate them due to their predation on domestic fowl, so bounties were placed on them in many places. Both forces took a heavy toll on the animals, but as trapping became regulated and commercial fox farms began producing more pelts, fewer wild animals were captured. The bounty system proved unsatisfactory, and eventually all states ceased the practice. And finally, farmers learned how to fox-proof their chicken pens, so that form of opposition all but vanished.

The red fox is the largest of the species, attaining weights of up to 15 pounds. Most often, they display the color which gave them their name, a golden red. This dominates the upper parts from its black nose to the end of its bushy, white-tipped tail. The belly, chin and throat are white, and the feet, backs of the ears and sometimes parts of the tail are black. There are silver, black, brown and intermediate color phases, but all have the white-tipped tail.

The red fox is omnivorous, and it ingests a very wide variety of foods. During the summer months it eats berries, grapes, cherries, apples, peaches,

Want to see what's going on at night? Bausch & Lomb's Night Vision binoculars make it possible to see coyotes, foxes, and bobcats coming in.

cantaloupe, corn, grasses, acorns and a variety of invertebrates that includes beetles, grasshoppers, crickets, caterpillars, salamanders, and crayfish. They prey on rabbits, woodchucks, squirrels, quail, pheasants and various other kinds of birds, and rodents year-around, but these are the main food sources during the winter months. Also, as noted, given the chance it will snatch up a chicken or any other kind of domestic fowl.

Dens are used only for maternity purposes, and these may be located in caves, hollow trees or logs, rock and brush piles, or in excavations they create on hillsides or along stream banks. Mounds of dirt covering food caches are usually close by. Mating takes place in January and February, with litters of from one to 10 born from 51 to 53 days later. The kits begin to emerge from the dens at about 1 month of age and disperse at 4 months, and the den is abandoned.

In the winter red foxes usually sleep in the open, curled up into a ball with the bushy tail acting as a blanket. They remain comfortable even when covered by snow, and often they burrow into it for added warmth and protection. Much of their foraging is done at night, but in lean times they move about as readily in daylight hours. Their shy, wary nature causes them to be very secretive, seldom being seen even by people living near their habitat.

The range covers all of Canada except small parts of British Columbia and Saskatchewan, and all but the extreme northern parts of Alaska. In the U.S., they're found everywhere except for southwestern California, Utah,

Nevada, Arizona, northwest Texas, and the coastal region from North Carolina to Florida.

Experts say the red fox population is at an estimated three or four million and will continue to expand unless competition with the coyote blocks or slows its growth.

Although the showy red fox is the species most familiar to the public, a close look at the smaller gray fox reveals an animal that easily matches it in grace and beauty. The upper parts are a grizzled gray, and the underparts and back of the head reddish. The throat is white, and the feet rusty colored. The tail is black on top, with a black tip. Weights are from 7 to 13 pounds.

The gray fox is also more versatile, since it has tree-climbing ability. This allows it to harvest fruits and nuts before they fall and can be eaten by ground-bound animals. Grays often take refuge in trees when pursued, or use them as resting places.

Like the red fox, it is omnivorous, with a major part of its diet consisting of cottontail rabbits, rats, mice, voles, and many other small mammals and birds. Various kinds of plant material are eaten, including grasses, persimmons, grapes, apples, cherries, blackberries, acorns, pokeweed fruit, and strawberries. They also forage for insects, salamanders, small snakes, and crayfish. Gray foxes don't have red foxes' notoriety for stealing chickens, but occasional cases of missing domestic fowl can be traced to them.

Dens are most often in natural openings such as rock crevices, caves, abandoned woodchuck burrows, hollow trees or logs, rock and brush piles or under boulders. They sometimes will den under abandoned farm buildings. The dens are used all winter for shelter and safety, and most often the same sites are used year after year, either by the same animals or succeeding generations.

Mating takes place in February and March, with litters of from two to seven pups born in March or April. The young are weaned in three months and are on their own in four months.

The gray fox range is almost entirely in the U.S., with only a couple of small intrusions into Canada. They occupy the entire eastern states west to North and South Dakota, Nebraska, Kansas, Oklahoma. They're also found in most of Texas, New Mexico, Arizona, California, and eastern Oregon, the southern parts of Utah, and Nevada, and Colorado. There is one species related to the gray fox, The Insular Gray Fox, which occurs as six subspecies on six islands off the California coast.

The arctic fox changes colors with the seasons, going from brown to white as winter begins as a means of matching the environment. An uncommon blue phase is a dark blue-gray in summer, and a pale blue-gray in winter.

This animal of the far North, and typical of all creatures that inhabit deserts, hot or frigid, has special physical attributes. The most obvious are the short legs and compact body that help to reduce heat loss, and the thick fur that helps to contain it. It also has hairy footpads that provide both insulation and traction on icy surfaces.

Arctic foxes eat almost anything they can catch, find or steal. Lemmings are a main food source in the summer, along with young arctic or snowshoe hares, the eggs and young of birds, fish, berries, and some plant material. In winter they depend heavily on carrion, and they follow polar bears in order to scavenge the leftovers from their kills. It isn't unusual for these animals to forage for distances as much as a thousand miles. At times when food is abundant, it is stored in holes dug into the permafrost.

The range of the Arctic fox extends from northern and western Alaska into Canada south to the Northwest Territories, and into northern Alberta, Manitoba, and Quebec. Its principal enemy is the trapper, but with the decrease in fur sales, the population has risen sharply. This has caused more serious depredation on nesting waterfowl and other birds which nest within its range.

There are two other fox species that are sometimes linked together, but differences in ranges and physical characteristics make it clear that they are not the same.

The Kit Fox is a small, slender animal, yellowish in color, with large ears and a black-tipped tail. Its range is fairly broad, extending south from southeastern Oregon and including parts of California, Nevada, Utah, New Mexico, and Texas. It is also found in western and central Mexico.

The kit fox eats small rodents, insects, berries, lizards, and snakes. Man seldom seeks it, and its natural enemies are eagles and coyotes.

The Swift Fox is a creature of the high plains and prairies, and one of the fastest of all of the foxes. Tawny colored, with a black-tipped tail, it bears a close resemblance to the kit fox. Both weigh from 3 to 6 pounds, and as its name implies, the swift fox is also very fast.

The range extends from southern Alberta, Saskatchewan and Manitoba southward, including the eastern half of Montana and Wyoming, eastern Colorado, northeastern New Mexico, northwestern Texas, all of North Dakota, South Dakota and Nebraska, the extreme western parts of Minnesota and Iowa, and western Kansas and Oklahoma.

Rabbits, mice, rats, squirrels and other small rodents are mainstay diet items, along with birds, snakes, lizards, berries, nuts and other vegetable matter.

Destruction of swift fox habitat threatened its existence for a time, but it is now protected in some areas as an endangered species and is holding its own.

HUNTING METHODS

To most, the mention of foxes brings to mind people attired in red coats, white breeches and polished boots riding on horseback behind hounds hot on the trail of their quarry, or a group of overall-clad men sitting around a campfire telling tall tales and listening to the exciting bugling of the foxhounds coursing through the nearby woodlands. And maybe taking an occasional swing from a jug to ward off the real or imagined chill of the night.

Varmint hunters see foxes in a different way, since they have to compete with them on even terms. Even though the intelligence of foxes doesn't compare with coyotes, they're far from being slouches where wariness and cunning are concerned. Plenty of hunters have had the experience of being thoroughly duped by foxes, and those who haven't are almost certain to have it in their future.

Trapping and following the hounds once accounted for the majority of foxes taken, but once predator calling came onto the scene, the situation changed dramatically. Varmint hunters have become proficient in the art of luring them in, and this has broadened the scope of the sport.

In the northern states where winter snow is dependable, certain conditions make it possible to trail foxes and overtake them. Red foxes carry their tails low, and when traveling in wet or melting snow, the tails accumulate a load of slush and ice, the weight of which eventually exhausts the animals. Without strength to continue, the foxes become easy prey for a hunter.

Hunting bedded foxes in the snow is another popular method, which requires finding tracks and following them to where a fox is nestled down in the snow. Because walking in the snow, and especially in crusty snow, is noisy, a very stealthy approach is necessary. A better tactic is to call, arouse the animal and coax it in.

Another still hunting technique is to locate the trails foxes routinely use when foraging and wait for them to appear. Since foxes are primarily nocturnal, the early morning and late afternoon periods are the daylight times when they are most likely to be seen.

Many of the same sounds used to attract coyotes and bobcats work well on both the gray and red species, although they have their own peculiarities and habits that make hunting them a specific art. Also, different tactics are required for each because they don't usually occupy the same kinds of habitat. It's not possible to cover all of the details involved in the predator calling game in this volume, but there's a book that can fully explain the mysteries a beginner encounters: *Murray Burnham's Hunting Secrets* is the predator caller's bible and is an invaluable reference for both novice and experienced hunters.

If you're in a place where night hunting is permitted, this is by far the most productive period, and moonless nights are always the best. Foxes are nocturnal and on the prowl for food, which makes them especially susceptible to calls imitating the prey they seek. Since foxes don't try to bring down ani-

When night hunting, a good spotlight is necessary. This hand-held Coleman spotlight produces an amazing one million candlepower.

This Nite Lite mounts on the barrel or scope and can be turned on at the last minute to il-luminate the target.

mals larger than themselves, the distress sounds of rabbits or mouse squeaks are the most effective.

In night calling for foxes and all other species, the light used to illumi-nate the hunting zone should remain on at all times, since turning it on and off can be distracting to both the hunter and the quarry. A red or orange light doesn't frighten foxes, regardless of how it's directed, but the beam of a white light should be kept above ground level. There are many ways to manipulate a beam, some of them relating to whether it's operated from a vehicle or from a hunter's headlight. The best combination is a red light for seeing the animal's eyes, and a white light mounted on the gun barrel that can be turned on when it's time to shoot.

Scouting areas you plan to hunt is important in deciding where to set up after darkness. Fox sign is similar to that of coyotes, but because foxes are much smaller and lighter, their tracks are usually very difficult to discern. The scat usually contains hair, since rodents are a principal food source, but if this is absent, it can mean that they are feeding mostly on other things. Rodents mean open spaces, while other contents may suggest wooded or brushy locations, and it will assist in deciding where to position yourself. Foxes are much more inclined to use the same game routes of travel, which are usually game and livestock trails and country roads, and the amount of scat found at these locations is a measure of the number of foxes that are in the vicinity.

The Winchester Model 70 in .22–250 with a Bausch & Lomb 6X–24X and a pair of Bausch & Lomb Elite binoculars are excellent for fox hunting.

EQUIPMENT AND ACCESSORIES

Since foxes can be called into close range, especially at night, a shotgun is the best choice. The animal's bushy fur makes it look a lot bigger than it really is, and the chances of missing it or not hitting a vital spot with a rifle in semi-darkness are very high. A full-choked 12 gauge shotgun loaded with high brass or magnum shells and No. 2 or No. 4 shot sizes will do the job very well. If a rifle is preferred, the .17 Remington, .22 Hornet, .25–20 Winchester and .32–20 Winchester are good choices.

Foxes often respond to calls very quickly, so electronic calls aren't recommended. Manual types are better, since the tones and volume can be matched to the situation and the animal's reactions.

At times, insects can be a problem at night, and repellents can be useful. However, care should be taken to select a type with a scent that won't be a handicap. There's an earth scent repellent that's very satisfactory for all types of game where the olfactory element is a factor.

9

BOBCATS

Of the seven members of the cat family found in North America, only one, the Bobcat or "wildcat," is given serious consideration by varmint hunters. The main reason for this may be their wide distribution and the great capacity they display in being able to adapt to changing environmental conditions.

This cat's common name isn't hard to figure: with the exception of its cousin, the Lynx, it is the only native feline with a short, stubby tail. Unlike some domestic dogs that display this trademark, the bobcat's is a natural feature. Normally, this appendage is very important in maintaining balance in climbing and leaping, yet the bobcat seems to manage both of these actions quite well despite its absence.

Although there are some variations from one location to another, the basic color of the bobcat is pale to reddish-brown with indistinct black spots and streaks above, and a whitish color below. The tail is black above and white below, and the ears slightly tufted. Weights vary fairly widely, generally

This hunter took a 35-pound female bobcat while hunting a steeply sloped area in New York's Catskill Mountains.

ranging from 14 to 40 pounds, but specimens of up to 69 pounds have been recorded. Males are larger than the females. In size, they are from 28 to 49 inches long.

Part of the differences in sizes and weights reflect the type of country in which they're found, but genetic differences are also responsible for these variations. Throughout the United States there are nine subspecies, each of which exhibits some specific identifying characteristics.

The bobcat is a very efficient hunter, and meat is the primary item in its diet. Rabbits, squirrels, mice, rats, porcupines and a variety of other rodents, small mammals, and birds are included, as well as domestic fowl. Its strength is indicated by the fact that a big adult bobcat can bring down an antelope or a full-grown deer. Carrion is eaten only on rare occasions. With the rapidly increasing wild turkey populations across the country, both the young and adult birds have become a favorite target of this cat. Some hunting is done from trees, where it perches and waits for prey to appear, but it operates mostly on the ground. The mottled fur is an excellent camouflage that permits them to blend easily into most woodland backgrounds.

Normally, if food availability is good and little hunting pressure is exerted, a bobcat's range size can be as small as five miles in diameter, yet otherwise it may be as much as 50 miles.

Many of the calls bobcats make are sometimes mistaken for those of house cats, although not their high, piercing scream, which has been likened to that of a terrified woman.

Bobcats use thickets, caves, and brush piles as hiding places during the day, conducting most of their hunting at night. At times when food is scarce, they will also forage during the daylight hours. They are good swimmers, but they usually enter the water only when pursued and no other alternative escape route exists. Areas with scrubby or second-growth forests and fairly rugged terrain are favored habitat, but they also adapt well to mountainous areas and swamps. The shyness and stealth of the bobcat permit it to live close to populated areas without the residents' ever being aware of its presence. At times they compete with raccoons and opossums for dog and cat food left on back porches or the yards of houses.

Breeding takes place in the spring, with a litter of usually from two to four born in late April or early May. Once the female is close to giving birth, she drives the male away, because he is likely to devour the young: the helpless

Bobcat

kittens are too tempting and easy a meal to pass up. Maternity dens are likely to be in hollow logs, dense brush piles or rock shelters. The young begin hunting with their mother at about 7 months, then become independent at about 9 to 12 months.

There are records of crosses between bobcats and house cats, but this occurs rarely.

Adults lead solitary lives except during the mating season, and males and females have separate territories that seldom overlap. Like many animals, they urinate on rocks or trees to establish scent posts defining their sector of operations, and often the scat also serves this purpose. Bobcats are very fastidious in regard to burying their fecal matter. There's an Indian legend that expresses the belief that such deposits eventually turn into precious jewels, which is why they're so well concealed. However, why this would be of concern to the bobcat is impossible to fathom.

The bobcat ranges from coast to coast across the U.S. and into Mexico and the extreme southern parts of all of the Canadian provinces. The highest populations exist in the western states, but since intensive trapping of the animals has diminished, they are making good comebacks in many of the eastern states. The only region where they are conspicuously absent is in the central to lower Midwest. Enemies of adult animals other than man are wolves, coyotes and domestic dogs. Foxes and horned owls sometimes prey upon kittens. At one time there was a strong demand for bobcat fur, and trappers vigorously sought the animals. Today, with the prices down, there are much fewer taken in this manner.

Closely associated with the bobcat in appearance and habits is the Lynx, but its range and habits cause it to be of only minor interest to varmint hunters. However, it's a worthy adversary, because it possesses all of the stealth and elusiveness of its close cousin.

The range of the lynx includes all of Canada and Alaska except the extension of the Great Plains that lie in southern Alberta, Saskatchewan, and Manitoba. In the U.S. it occupies only parts of Washington, northern Oregon and Idaho, a very small part of Montana, and a few Rocky Mountain locations in Wyoming and Colorado. Northern Wisconsin, Minnesota, and Michigan have populations. In the East, a few are found in northern New England and New York.

Well adapted to its northern range, the lynx is heavily furred, including its feet, which allows it to move silently and rapidly through the snow. Its color is a tawny buff, with brownish underparts. Its tail is short, but longer than the bobcat's, and it has tufted ears and pale cheek ruffs that form a beard at the throat. Males are larger than the females and may weigh up to 60 pounds.

Mostly nocturnal, the lynx stays hidden by day under fallen trees, low-hanging evergreen limbs or rock ledges. Like the bobcat, it is an expert climber and often hunts from trees. Snowshoe hares are its principal prey, although a variety of small rodents and mice are also mainstays. The remains of large game animals—moose, caribou, sheep and deer—supply food in the winter months. It caches leftovers under snow for future meals. Livestock are sometimes targets of the lynx, but this usually occurs on farms in remote areas.

Man has long been a major enemy of the lynx, since its long, silky fur has been of prime market value. Wolves and mountain lions are its only other threat.

The tawny-colored Mountain Lion, also known as Puma, Cougar, Panther, and Catamount, is the largest of North American purring cats, weighing up to 275 pounds. While it is the most widely distributed, its numbers are far below those of the bobcat, but this has not always been the case. Once, the mountain lion was found from coast to coast and from British Columbia to South America. A superior predator capable of killing large animals, wild and domestic, it became a number one enemy of cattle and sheep ranchers early on, and later of game officials in some places. As a result, their numbers and range have been reduced enormously. While still hunted in areas where they are abundant, they are fully protected in most states in which only small populations remain.

The major concentrations of mountain lions are presently found from British Columbia and southern Alberta south into Mexico, including parts of Washington, Oregon, California, Montana, Idaho, Wyoming, Utah, Colorado, Arizona, New Mexico, and Texas. Limited populations occur in Louisiana, Tennessee, Alabama and Florida.

There have only been a few sightings of Jaguar in the U.S. since the late 1940s, but this beautiful spotted cat once occupied a territory that included southeastern and central California, and southern Arizona, New Mexico, and Texas. Attaining weights of up to 300 pounds, it is an extremely powerful and efficient predator. Because it preys on livestock, and its fur is of great value, the jaguar has been heavily reduced in numbers in its major range, which extends from Mexico into South America.

Three other cats with primary ranges south of the Mexican border, and which American varmint hunters likely will never see, are the Ocelot, Jaguarundi and Margay.

The ocelot is the largest of the trio, attaining weights of up to 40 pounds. The tawny-gold body is covered with lines of brown, black-bordered markings: rosettes, bars, rings and specks. Once fairly abundant in the range they occupied in the U.S., they preyed on small livestock, which prompted efforts at eradication. Habitat loss also contributed, as did hunting them for their pelts.

Ocelots are fully protected over their present range, which includes southern Oklahoma, southwest Arkansas, western Louisiana, Texas, and a small corner of southeastern Arizona.

The long, slim jaguarundi weighs from 15 to 18 pounds, and appears in three color phases: all black, all gray, and russet with a white underside. When animals of different colors breed, the young may be of mixed hues.

The only places in the U.S. where they have been known to occur are extreme southern Texas and extreme southeast Arizona.

The last margay sighting in this country was in Texas in the mid-1800s, and less is known about this small, 5–to–7–pound cat than any of its relatives, even in its primary range from Mexico to Argentina. It is known that it has exceptional climbing ability, and can descend a tree headfirst, a feat the other cats can't accomplish. Margays are thought to be mostly nocturnal, with an extremely secretive nature which makes observing their habits very difficult.

HUNTING METHODS

One of the earliest forms of hunting bobcats for sport dates back to Colonial times when dog packs were used to pursue and tree them. It's an exciting and exhilarating technique that reached its peak of perfection with the use of the Kentucky foxhound, since this breed seems to adapt more to bobcats than any of the others. One of the main qualities required in a 'cat hound is a good nose, because this animal leaves less scent in its travels than any of the other cats. Bobcats are also extremely tricky when being trailed, using the tactic of doubling back on their track.

Dogs will usually tree a bobcat, but occasionally it bays and gives dogs a fierce fight.

Bagging one of these animals without use of dogs or other devices can result in pretty slim pickings, and most bobcats taken under such circumstances are killed incidental to deer or turkey hunting. It's a case of two predators seeking the same prey at the same place.

If dog packs and incidental kills were the only way gun hunters could bag bobcats, the numbers they harvested would be quite small. However, there's another way to go about it that can pay big dividends, depending upon the skills of the individual involved: the use of predator calls.

Calling techniques that attract bobcats don't differ greatly from those used for other predators, except for the fact that the old saying about curiosity and cats applies, and calls unrelated to food often bring them in as quickly as ones that hold the promise of a meal. Too, because bobcats will make a run at prey many times larger than themselves, calling sounds don't have to be restricted to those emitted by the smaller creatures.

Also, the behavior of called bobcats is very unpredictable. Most of the time they approach cautiously, with the typical cat tactics of slow, deliberate movement, taking advantage of any type of cover available. They possess keen vision,

Many bobcats are killed incidentally by deer hunters. This one substituted for a buck on an Alabama hunt.

This Game Tracker pop-up blind provides plenty of room for two hunters, and full 360-degree visibility. It's also a nice haven in the rain.

which is particularly acute at night since their eyes are designed to operate better in low light conditions; and their hearing is equally sharp. They depend on these two characteristics the most, since their sense of smell isn't particularly good. If the least bit suspicious, they will either abandon the stalk and vanish, or stop and sit awhile to think things over. Patience is required on the part of the hunter because even if the animal stops, all isn't lost. Sometimes all it takes to get it interested again is to switch to another kind of call. If a nonfood kind brought it in, a mouse squeak or subdued rabbit distress call may do the trick.

Bobcats are shy and furtive, spending the daylight hours in dense cover sleeping or resting. The main activity is at night, when they will roam out in open areas seeking the rabbits and rodents that are the major part of their diet year around. This is why night hunting is so much more productive for these animals. Bobcats can be called in the daytime, but they're so sneaky and elusive that they may be in close without the caller's ever seeing them.

In scouting for bobcats, the best places to look for tracks and scat are along stream banks, around ponds or water holes and in brushy or second-growth areas. Once enough sign is discovered to make a hunt feasible, the next step is to find the closest location that provides an open space where you can set up to hunt after nightfall. Ideally, you want a spot without any cover so that the bobcat has no avenue of approach on which it can't be seen. Otherwise, you may have cats come and go without ever being aware of their presence. It also helps to have some elevation, whether it be from the back of the truck, in a tree or on a natural rise in the terrain, since this makes it easier to spot bobcats that come sneaking in. If the place chosen isn't devoid of cover, one way to cause the animal to come in without a kill on its mind is to use one of the nonfood calls.

There's a particular satisfaction in bagging bobcats, mainly because of the reputation cats have of being so mysterious and ghost-like in their movements. This really isn't true. Bobcats are no more difficult to lure than any of the other predators, and possibly less so than some. Still, the sensation always seems to be present, and enjoying it does no harm.

EQUIPMENT AND ACCESSORIES

Both rifles and shotguns can be used on bobcats. The choice sometimes depends on whether or not you want to keep the pelt. A rifle will put a single hole in the hide, whereas a shotgun will make it a sieve.

Gerber's Sport Utility Pack is designed as an emergency kit for off-road vehicles, and contains a hatchet, folding shovel, flashlight, Multi-Plier, and folding saw.

One of the favorite bobcat cartridges is the .243 Winchester, but the .25–06 Remington and 6mm Remington are also popular. The smaller .22 center-fires like the .222 Remington and .223 Remington are very effective, too, but anything below this level ballistically isn't recommended. As for shotguns, a 12 gauge loaded with No. 4 buckshot is quite sufficient. Bobcats are tough creatures, and nobody wants to tangle with a crippled one. Those familiar with these animals realize that the old saying referring to a man that can "whip his weight in bobcats" meant that a very formidable person was being discussed!

Accessories are much the same as those used for coyotes and foxes.

10

CROWS

The crow is a member of a family that also includes ravens, jays and magpies, all bold, aggressive birds whose behavior patterns range from simply annoying to highly destructive. The crow occupies the last category, which has caused it to be a principal target for varmint hunters, as well as farmers and others who become victims of these birds' activities. A band of these large, strong birds can create havoc on whatever they descend upon.

The Common Crow occupies almost all of North America except the far northern regions. It breeds from Newfoundland south to Florida, and west across Canada, and winters across the U.S. and south into Mexico and beyond. In areas with moderate climates, crows don't migrate.

Crows are present almost everywhere—forests, fields, parks, and suburban areas. Seeing them in inner city areas is not uncommon. They operate from central positions, large roost sites at which they gather in late afternoon, following travel lanes back from wherever they have been feeding during the day. These roosts may harbor thousands of birds, and they're favorite locations

Crow

at which gunners can waylay them. Shortly after dawn they are back on the move again, usually using the same travel lanes as they radiate back out over the countryside.

As omnivorous birds, crows eat almost anything, so their diet includes all kinds of vegetable, insect and animal matter, including carrion. Garbage dumps attract crows, and they have a great fondness for field crops.

Crows do extensive environmental damage, and one of the most prominent examples is the severe impact their predation has annually on waterfowl populations. It's proof of how ruthlessly destructive these birds can be. When the hens begin laying, the crows invade the nests and break open and eat the eggs. Later, when the hatches occur, they devour the fledglings. The degree of devastation is incalculable, but it's obvious it significantly decreases the number of birds that migrate down the flyways each fall.

Crows take a heavy toll on upland game birds and songbirds in the same manner, and they also prey on the young of small game animals, such as rabbits and squirrels. Few predators can match them when it comes to destroying wildlife. Every hunter has witnessed crows being harassed in flight by smaller birds, which is evidence that they are regarded as natural enemies.

Like the coyote, the crow possesses a highly developed mentality, and experts say it has reached the furthest stage yet achieved by any avian species. It has a solid social organization and a communication system that is both complex and extremely effective, attributes that help explain the crow's wariness and cunning. It also possesses great predatory skills, and in many ways this raucous, bold thief is a feathered version of its canine counterpart in environmental crime.

There are other things these two varmints share. Each has been the target of massive efforts aimed at total eradication of the species. They have been poisoned, their roosts bombed, bounties placed on them, and intense gunning pressure applied, yet they have endured and emerged as another example of the ultimate in survival tactics.

Due to changes in agricultural practices and other factors, crow populations across the country aren't as large as they once were; but they're plentiful enough to afford varmint hunters lots of shooting. There used to be no closed season on crows anywhere in the country, but now the U.S. Fish and Wildlife Service has ruled that each state must establish a closed season during the nesting period.

The crow's intelligence has given rise to many myths, one of which is that crows "hold court" and judge individual members of the clan for misdeeds. Some also believe that they descend upon offenders found guilty and either kill them or drive them away.

They do display other "smart" characteristics, though. Sometime sentinels are posted to watch fields in which they are feeding, and there's evidence that scouts are sent out in advance of feeding forays to check for danger. Crows also will drop clams, oysters or other hard-shelled prey on rocks to break them open, and they drop hickory nuts and black walnuts on highways and let passing vehicles do the cracking.

The practice of "mobbing" hawks and owls has long been observed, and often large numbers of birds participate in these attacks on their enemies. What is sometimes mistaken for mobbing of an individual crow is nothing more than the other birds' attempting to rob it of some choice food item it has obtained. It's a sort of aerial hijacking.

The crow also has a rather special distinction. During World War II it was designated as an enemy of the American public and was the subject of a widespread propaganda campaign. The message was that these "black bandits," were robbing the nation's farms of grain that was vitally needed for the production of food for both civilians and the military. Hunters were urged to destroy crows at every opportunity as a contribution to the war effort; and spurred on by patriotism, they went at it with a vengeance. Farmers had the priority in purchasing the limited supply of shotgun shells and .22 cartridges allotted to sporting goods and hardware stores.

There's no way to gauge the result of this crusade, but it's doubtful that its impact on the crow population was significant. Most of the men who were active hunters were in the armed forces, so the number of people participating in the extermination attempt wasn't massive, by any means. After the war, the crow population was more than adequate to keep hunters actively involved in the sport. What the wartime campaign did mainly was focus attention briefly on a sport that had been practiced since the late 1800s when shooting these pesky birds became popular.

In the early years when agriculture was the major part of the nation's economy, conditions were ideal for supporting large crow populations. Huge numbers of the birds were present in some locations, especially in the farm belt states. At such places, some of the roosts attracted hundreds of thousands of crows. Shoots with lots of participants were often held at these sites, resulting in big kills, but even two or three hunters could count on bagging as many as several hundred birds in a day.

There were, and still are, crow-shooting contests held, with the winners eventually competing in a world championship. The interest isn't as intense as in years past, but the devotees are just as enthusiastic. Crow hunting is a special kind of sport, and there will always be hunters who will eagerly accept the challenges they offer.

Two other kinds of crows exist in North America, but both have very restricted ranges. Neither poses the environmental threat of the common crow, since their numbers are much smaller.

The Fish Crow inhabits seashores, estuaries, and large river valleys from New England to Florida and around the Gulf Coast to Texas. Its main source of food is fish, shoreline jetsam and various plants and berries found in the areas.

On the other side of the continent, the Northwestern Crow occupies a thin strip of range from Washington to Alaska. It occasionally feeds on croplands, but more often it scavenges along the seashores to obtain most of the items it eats.

HUNTING METHODS

A beginner who is considering taking up crow shooting as a sport must first realize that, like many other forms of hunting, it isn't as simple as it might seem. Crows are deceptive, and just because they don't seem to be especially wary when approached without a gun or in a threatening manner doesn't mean they're easy targets. As indicated, crows are extremely intelligent birds that always seem to be well aware of the intentions of people who come near them. Veteran hunters swear that they can tell the difference between a hand-held farm or garden implement and a gun. Some also believe that crows can count, so if four hunters enter a blind and two leave, the birds don't let their guard down. They know two are left inside. There's no absolute proof of this, but considering all of the other sophisticated faculties crows possess, it's worth thinking about.

Successful crow hunting is a combination of several factors, and while certain ones may seem more significant than others, they're actually highly interdependent. Put together properly, they're consistently unbeatable.

Mouth calls are the most widely used crow lures, and there are many models available from which to choose.

With this in mind, regard what follows as having nothing to do with levels of importance.

The vast majority of crow hunters are shotgunners who rely on calling to lure the birds, and as vital as this aspect is to the sport, how they're used is also critical. It's true than a rank amateur can attract crows' attention, and perhaps even knock some down. However, this is a rudimentary approach compared with the tactics and strategies necessary for conducting a shoot where hundreds of birds may be killed.

The way to begin is at a sporting goods store, where you select a crow call that is accompanied by an instructional tape or video. This will allow you to learn all of the basics before going into the field. Once done, go to a place that crows frequent, hear how they "talk," then go home and try to mimic the sounds. The ones to which you should pay the most attention are the hail calls and those which indicate excitement or alarm.

Better still, go with a veteran crow hunter or team of hunters and listen to their repertoire of calls. These are the ones that are essential to successful crow hunting, since they're the ones that lure in, excite, and hold birds.

No doubt the original calling was done by mouth, and while there are still many hunters who can display this talent, nobody argues that greater efficiency and volume are produced by the manufactured kinds. These are reed-type calls, and while there are a great many models and styles on the market, they are basically the same. It all comes down to a matter of individual preference.

Crow calling is an art, and becoming proficient takes a lot of time and hunting experience. Crows can be easy to call one day and difficult the next, and calling repertoires should match different locations and situations. There's no single routine that can be used in all circumstances, and that's part of the challenge hunters face each trip into the field.

Individual calling can be effective, but a pair of hunters, or even a trio, can create a clamor that is greatly more compelling in stirring up the crows. Teams that have been working together for a long time have individual roles, so even though they're calling in unison, the sounds they make aren't the same. The idea is to make crows think they're hearing a chorus of excited and angry voices.

Two calls are musts:

The first is the fighting call that represents angry crows that have come upon an enemy and are furious. It is one that should be performed with much gusto, because this gets crows within hearing all fired up and ready for combat. The madder they get, the better the results.

The second call is the hail or comeback call that's used to lure birds that have strayed away back into the fray. This call should be sounded as soon as any birds begin to leave. They're vulnerable until they get a distance away and begin to cool off a bit.

Once a response is first elicited, hunters must keep their eye on the birds and watch how they respond and then make little alterations in their calling to keep them coming. As crows approach, the tempo is increased in order to build them into full frenzy, ready to take on whatever enemy is present. Having dozens of crows swirling overhead is the culmination of this kind of effort.

Since crows are loud and aggressive by nature, calling must match these characteristics. Don't hesitate to put everything into it, because there's no way you can out-shout these loudmouths. Most important is to establish a rhythm to build excitement and never pause.

One of the greatest boons to crow hunting was the development of the electronic call, which duplicates the sound of actual crow fights and clamor. These devices first appeared in the late 1950s and were immediately popular among hunters. They not only did a terrific job of attracting crows, but also permitted both hands to be free at all times. The first models were simply portable phonographs that were large and cumbersome, but over the years there have been dramatic improvements in both the size of the units and sound quality. One of today's electronic calls is computerized and pocket-size, and it can be programmed to play a variety of calls for use under different conditions.

These innovations didn't replace the old methods, by any means. Many hunters didn't wish to abandon the thrill and sense of accomplishment derived from standard calling procedures. To them it was turning their backs on skills that had taken years to perfect and which gave them a lot of satisfaction. Also, there's no question that electronic calls can't match traditional-style calling when it comes to versatility. There are many different situations encountered in crow hunting which require particular calling tactics, and in some of them it's necessary to quickly shift from one to the other.

Other hunters have gone one step further and integrated the mechanisms into the hunting routine. A commonly used tactic is to attract the crows by using standard calls, then turn on the electronic call when the birds start to

Electronic calls are very effective for crows. This hunter is placing a speaker outside the blind.

approach. From that point they can keep on calling if they wish to supplement the other sounds, or just get ready to shoot.

Okay, so step one is completed, and now it's time to move ahead. The question is: what are the birds supposed to be looking for? The answer is: whatever it is that has these "other crows" stirred up.

This is where decoys enter the picture.

A typical hunting setup will include an owl perched in a stand or in a tree, surrounded by crow decoys both in the trees and on the ground. Crows despise all raptors, but especially great horned owls. Most hunters who have spent a lot of time in the woods have witnessed crows harassing hawks or owls. Obviously, these birds raid crow nests, but whatever the reason may be, there's the equivalent of a blood feud between them.

Once approaching crows see the owl decoy, it's all over but the shooting. They will zero in on the predator and make swooping passes at it that give the hunter choice, close-range shots. When the birds are sufficiently aroused, they don't seem much bothered by the gunshots, especially if the hunters continue to call.

Once a few crows have been downed, they can be added to the decoys on the ground to make a more impressive spread. It's ordinary to have waves of crows coming to calls, allowing any blind or decoy adjustments to be made during lulls in the action.

Crow decoys can be as simple as profiles fashioned from plywood or cardboard and painted flat black. A stick can be attached to push into the ground and stand up the silhouettes. These work all right, but they're one-dimensional and can't be seen by birds directly overhead.

The better decoys are full-bodied, some cast in a hard plastic or fiber, and others that are made of a soft plastic and are light and flexible. It's important that some decoys in each set have a clothespin or other fixture that will attach them to tree limbs or barbed wire fences. The owl is always placed well above ground level, and it's best to have some decoys in the immediate area around it.

Sometimes half a dozen decoys are enough, but having up to a couple of dozen makes the scene even more compelling in the eyes of the crow.

Camouflaged clothing is absolutely essential for successful crow shooting, and it should be as complete as possible. That means head-to-toe coverage, including hands, and particularly the face. A naked face flashes like a mirror in the light, and it can spook crows from as much as a quarter- to half-mile away. Their eyesight is much more keen than that of humans, and any little flaw in a setup can spell disaster. Many times crows will send a single bird to a calling site to scout the area. It usually passes out of gun range, and if everything is right it returns to give the okay to the others.

The great horned owl decoy represents one of the crow's most hated enemies; it's a sure-fire decoy when accompanied by good calling.

An owl decoy and a few crow decoys can produce lively shooting.

Crows detect color very well, so this is a situation where red or blaze orange caps and other visible, brightly colored accessory items have to be avoided.

Face masks bother some shooters, in which case camouflaged grease-paint can be substituted. This same substance can be applied to the hands if gloves are also a hindrance. Having a camouflaged shotgun provides the final touch in becoming invisible.

Staying hidden and steady calling will usually produce action.

Special attention must be paid to blinds, because regardless of how well camouflaged the hunter may be, it's almost impossible to perform satisfactorily without additional concealment. When a few or more hunters are involved, a blind supplies a central spot from which to operate and call.

At times, blinds can be fashioned from material found on the spot, but usually this takes a lot of time to accomplish. The commercial blinds are a far better idea, and they're more functional.

Placement of blinds is a key factor in bagging birds. First, they shouldn't be placed under trees, since this can handicap a hunter by obscuring overhead shots. Set it up in cover fairly near the decoys, making sure it's no higher than the vegetation in which it's placed. Otherwise it will stand out and crows will detect its presence.

Blinds should be placed a little upwind from the flyways crow use when they depart the roosts. In the meantime, if the wind shifts, change the position of the blind so you are still using it to your best advantage. That's one reason why the portable blinds are advisable. An alternative is to build several blinds at the location just to be sure you're backed up in case of wind direction changes.

Finding the best places to shoot crows requires some scouting and inquiries. A roost is a principal clue, because once you know their evening destination, it's a rather simple matter to identify the major flyways on which they travel when fanning out over the countryside in the mornings. The places they have chosen to feed may be many miles away, and it's not necessary to know where these are. If you happen to be at one of them, all the better. What's most important is to be able to position yourself somewhere along a flyway so you'll

Pop-up blinds can give you a real edge on wary crows.

be certain of having birds within hearing and visual distance of your setup. Crows may be on their way to breakfast, but they seldom pass up the opportunity to join in what they perceive as a brawl that's underway.

The same thing doesn't hold true in the evenings when they're returning to the roost. Calling may cause a few birds to deviate from their path, but it's seldom that a high degree of excitement can be generated. Pausing takes time, and when the light is failing, they're anxious to get situated in the roost before darkness falls.

Roving hunters can almost always find spots where a quick setup will result in action, although the chances of collecting more than a dozen or so birds is usually minimal. This hopscotch method is useful when there's no hot spot available. The way to do it is to ride along back roads, stopping occasionally to call. A strong response can often signal the presence of crows looking for a fight, which can become a little bonanza for the hunters.

Few sports are better for training a person in wing shooting techniques than crow hunting. First of all, you get the chance to do plenty of shooting, and some of the birds don't pose much of a challenge. Those are the "starters" that help build confidence, but on the other end of the spectrum there are the fast, tricky birds that perform aerial maneuvers that can baffle even veteran gunners. Wind gives them even more of an advantage, because their large, powerful wings and broad "rudder" tail permits them to do amazing things. They can sail, hover, plummet like a rock, flare wildly, do snap rolls or use a tailwind to flash past a hunter at speeds resembling a jet fighter on a strafing run. Once witnessed, these aerobatics will cause any wing shooter to grant them extra respect!

Some of the toughest shooting crow hunters can experience is at roosts. The idea here is to position a number of hunters around a site in late afternoon and wait for the birds to arrive. There's no calling or decoys involved. When the birds arrive, they're dedicated to getting settled down into the trees before nightfall, and shooting doesn't deter them. Often the roost sites are in pine thickets, and with crows swirling overhead and diving into the roost from all directions, the action is fast and furious. It's almost as if the hunters are protecting the site against attacking birds. Since this begins to occur shortly before dark, it doesn't last long, but it's an unforgettable gunning experience.

Because of the short-range shooting, this is one situation in which an improved cylinder bore will get better results.

Yet while the shotgun is the principal crow-hunting weapon, there's a fraternity of varmint hunters who prefer to use rifles to pick off the birds at long range. This doesn't provide the same hot-and-heavy action, but that's not what's expected. Instead, exploding a crow at 200 or 300 yards with a high-intensity cartridge such as a .220 Swift or a-.22–250 Remington derives the enjoyment. And with these loads, exploding is a literal term!

There's a significant challenge, too, in that despite the crows' appearance of being fairly large, the actual body size is relatively small. It takes precision shooting to hit them at long range.

This is a relaxing form of hunting, and a favorite way to go about it is to cruise back roads and spot birds sitting in trees or feeding in fields. In places where it's legal to shoot from vehicles, the hunter doesn't even have to expose himself: crows aren't spooky about cars or trucks, but once a human form emerges, they go on full alert. Those who hunt in this manner often have rifle rests and spotting scopes mounted on the doors so no outside setups are needed. Shooting across the hood or top of a car, resting the rifle on sandbags, is a common practice. Care must be taken that the muzzle of the rifle is positioned so the blast doesn't scar or burn the paint job.

There are certain times that are especially good for picking off crows using this tactic. They like to scrounge in newly plowed ground for worms and grubs, and they can also be counted on to be there whenever grain is being planted. Another prime time is just after a snowstorm when the ground is covered. Crows are very active when searching for food, and they're very easy to spot. If you can locate manure piles, you have a winner, because these are natural magnets for the birds.

One of the main challenges faced is that crows on the ground are usually walking or hopping around most of the time. A bird will stop just long enough for the shooter to get the cross hairs on it, and then move just as the trigger is being squeezed. They're tough enough targets at long range without this kind of frustration. It's a good test of patience!

The use of decoys works well for riflemen, but the strategy is different. Sometimes simply placing a few crow decoys in the kind of field that would normally attract the birds will pay off. Another plan is to set a great horned owl decoy on a post or in a small tree along a fence line. In either of these situations, calling can be helpful, but since the shooter will be sitting a couple of hundred yards back from where the decoys are located, the only purpose is to get their at-

Crow silhouette decoys work fine when placed out in the open, since they appear to be feeding.

The pay-off: a crow bagged at 150 yards when it and some others flew in to join the decoys on the ground.

tention initially. Once they spot the decoys, calling should be discontinued because the distance between the caller and the decoys can cause confusion.

Plenty of crows can be killed using this technique, and as evidence, consider the case of Ray Weeks, of Tillsonburg, Ontario. His feats with a rifle are mentioned in Harvey Donaldson's classic bench rest and varmint shooter's book, *Yours Truly*, recently reprinted by Wolfe Publishing Company.

Donaldson states that during the middle 1930s, Weeks managed to bag from 4,500 to 5,000 crows every season! He worked for an insurance company, and his job was to drive around all over Ontario collecting payments. Most of his travels were in rural areas, and by carrying a rifle and ammunition with him at all times, he had lots of shooting opportunities. Donaldson says Weeks used the .22 Hornet chambered for his 2-R case, and the .219 Donaldson to attain his best records.

The odds are very much against totals like that ever again being achieved, but the anecdote may inspire some readers to give rifle hunting for crows a second thought.

Another productive approach is to find locations along the morning flyways that are target areas where some crows leave the flight and begin foraging. The shooter gets set up and waits for birds to sit down on the ground or in a tree.

Finally, there are those who prefer to stalk crows with a rifle using the basic .22 rimfire cartridge. This is similar to squirrel hunting, with the hunter sneaking through the woods and looking for crows sitting in the trees. A call can be used to good effect, either to lure birds or to determine their location and go after them. It's a technique many youngsters have used to bag their first crows and one that can be employed by any hunter as bonus action following a bushy-tail hunt.

EQUIPMENT AND ACCESSORIES

The 12 gauge shotgun is by far the most favored by crow hunters, because it is the most dependable killer. This gauge puts out a larger shot pattern than the 16 or 20 gauge, and it has greater range. Equipped with a set of choke tubes, it's practical for any situation, from high-flying birds that require full-choke patterns to birds that are diving in and coming within 25 yards. Modified or improved cylinder chokes are best for the task.

Twelve-gauge shotguns are the firearms of choice for crows.

There are those who favor 16 and 20 gauge guns, but few who go so far as to recommend the smaller .410 and 28 bores. Crows aren't hard to kill, but sometimes the ranges work against the smaller gauge guns, as well as the amount of lead they throw.

Picking the best kind of shells and shot sizes is more or less an individual choice, since both low brass and high brass are okay, and shot sizes from No. 4 to No. 8 will do the job. Crows aren't hard to knock down, so smaller shot provides more dense patterns. Many hunters use up shells from the previous hunting seasons, which may include a wide variety of loads.

Dedicated crow hunters burn up a lot of ammunition, so it's not surprising that a lot of them reload their shells. One big shoot with store-bought ammunition shells can be pretty costly, and even with reloading, it's not cheap!

Usually, crow hunters carry along several mouth-operated calls so as to have different sounds that are useful at particular times. Some have special long-range capabilities, while others are best when the birds are in close and the action is hot. There are many on the market from which to choose, although determining the right combination will require some experimenting in the field.

There are two major manufacturers of electronic calls, and both can create about every kind of crow sound that's ever been heard. One unit is worn on the belt and plays tiny phonograph records, but because of its limited volume, it's more practical for varmints other than crows.

Camouflage has been covered, but care should be taken to select the pattern most appropriate for the area where you hunt. Due to seasonal changes, it's wise to have several sets of garments, and since winter crow hunting can be very productive, having an all-white outfit is useful. Different weights of clothing are also needed at different times of the year.

Speaking of seasons, there are times when insect repellent or the impregnated mesh clothing mentioned in the chapter on squirrel hunting can be very useful in areas where mosquitoes, deer flies or other biting bugs abound.

One of the simplest of all is the one consisting of a long length of camouflaged cloth or mesh-plastic material with several long steel or aluminum poles that can be placed in the ground to establish preferred configuration. The material is then put in place. The whole operation can be performed in minutes. These are light, easily portable and can be quickly moved.

There are several pop-up-type blinds, and Game Tracker makes one with three panels that folds up and fits into a small cover that is light and portable. It gives a person plenty of room and several ports to see and shoot out of. There's also a double version that accommodates a pair of hunters. These offer total coverage of the hunter and are snug havens from wind and rain.

Nothing beats a good set of binoculars when it comes to locating concentrations of crows or cataloging their flyways. They also can permit a hunter to watch distant birds and determine their reaction to calls.

Long stays in a blind can be made more comfortable with either a light shooting seat or a cushion. There are many variations of these that are made especially for hunters, with camouflage and all.

Having a couple of large plastic trash bags will be helpful, because considerate hunters will sack up the dead birds, empty shells, shell boxes, and any other debris in order to leave the shooting site unlittered. The degree of courtesy that's exhibited by varmint hunters on private property often determines whether a return invitation will be issued, but the same practice should be followed on public lands, as well.

11

OTHER VARMINTS

It has been mentioned earlier that sometimes there's no exact set of guide-lines to determine what is and is not a varmint, but one thing is certain: there are literally dozens of bird and animals species that definitely can be placed in this category.

Some of these are found throughout the country, while others occupy more restricted ranges, and this causes the amount of interest to vary from intense to incidental according to location. However, because of the overall abundance and distribution of many of the species, it can be safely said that there's no place in North America where there's not at least one varmint available at any time of the year. The examples already listed would probably cover that claim, but there are plenty more to consider.

It is worth mentioning again that the regulations applying to varmints differ in the U.S. from state to state and in Canada from province to province, and special care must be taken to examine the rules in each location before going afield. In some instances, the species are under the jurisdiction of state laws, but others are protected under federal law. An example is the black-billed magpie, a destructive bird that plagues cattle and sheep ranchers in the western states. A 1972 amendment to the Migratory Bird Act of 1918 extended the blanket of protection to magpies, crows and some other species. Yet although crow hunting is still legal under loose seasonal restrictions, only persons holding a standing depredation permit can seek the magpie. This essentially eliminates varmint shooters from the picture unless the farmers and landowners in possession of a permit happen to enjoy the sport.

Exempted were three birds, each an exotic, and all of which are abundantly distributed throughout the country.

It would be hard to say which is the most familiar, but one stands out as the best sport for varmint shooters: the domestic pigeon.

There are few faster or trickier birds than pigeons, and even though the majority of them are city dwellers, there's plenty of opportunity to hunt them on farms. Sometimes the birds reside on the property, living in barns and other outbuildings, but urban pigeons quite commonly make flights out into the countryside to feed when grain is being planted or at harvest time. Landowners

Starling

have little use for these pests, and there's usually no trouble in gaining permission to shoot them.

Pigeon shooting can be fast and furious, and these birds can perform aerial maneuvers that would cause a jet pilot to turn green with envy. They're not easy to down, either, and most gunners go after them with 12 gauge shotguns and either beefed-up field loads or high brass shells. Another bonus is that they're good to eat, but because they have long life spans and can be tough, it's best to parboil them before beginning the final cooking process.

Calls don't work on pigeons, but decoys get good results, and there are commercial models available. Place them out in the field, and then add dead birds to the set to make it more attractive. The main feeding periods are from early- to midmorning and mid- to late afternoon. There's no season or limit imposed.

The starling is one of the most annoying and numerous of all North American vermin, yet few hunters go after it. It's a missed opportunity, since the starling can provide some of the best wing-shooting exercise that can be found. When the spring and fall migrations are under way and millions of birds are on the move, a hunter can take a stand beside a tree or on a hilltop and practice those shots that are troublesome during bird season. It beats skeet or trap shooting in terms of versatility, and it's also a great way to teach a youngster swing, lead and follow-through on flying targets.

The English sparrow used to be a major pest in urban areas, but with the passing of the horse as a means of conveyance, their numbers decreased rather dramatically. The birds depended upon horse manure as a major food source, and once this wasn't available, the population levels dropped. They are still nuisance birds and quite unimportant to adult varmint hunters, but they're significant, just the same. For many generations English sparrows were the first "game" young would-be hunters equipped with BB guns went after. As such they deserve mention, because they served a very useful purpose. Perhaps in some places, they still do.

Throughout the entire country, but particularly in the midwestern and northwestern regions, there are a great number of weasels, ground squirrels, chipmunks, pocket gophers, rats, mice, and voles that can be legally hunted and which provide varmint shooters with an immense amount of shooting opportunity. It's not wasted, either. In some of the mid-continent states, these little critters, some of which are nicknamed "picket pins" because of their up-

Shooting some of the small varmints at long range requires good optics and rifles that are extremely accurate.

right stances, supply a large percentage of the activity. Like prairie dogs, most of these animals are very prolific, so there's seldom any shortage of targets. Only a very few of the species are protected, the black-footed ferret being the most prominent example.

Some varmint hunters prefer small targets that require a greater emphasis on accuracy, and with the choices offered within the types of animals just listed, they can select whatever size they prefer. The little, but numerous, varmints offer another of the exciting ways that young or beginning hunters can be indoctrinated into the shooting game. Too, because they can be shot at either short or long ranges, the full gamut of calibers and cartridges can be used. The .22 rimfire is a good "starter," but even veteran shooters often continue to include the fancier, scope-equipped models in their stable of rifles used on the small varmints. This kind of hunting doesn't lend itself as well to long-range shooting as some of the others, mainly because the animals are too small to be seen at great distances. Cartridges with short- to mid-range capabilities are better, which makes the .17 Remington and .218 Bee perfect picks for this sport.

Pellet handguns and rifles are sufficient for smaller varmints. Shown from top are: Crossman .22-caliber pistol; Crossman .177-caliber pistol; Crossman .177-caliber rifle; Crossman .22-caliber rifle with 3x9x scope.

The badger is a tough, formidable burrower that is somewhat similar to the woodchuck, but with a much more aggressive and nastier temperament. It has a flattened body and short legs, with a white stripe from the shoulder to the tip of its upturned nose and white cheeks with a black patch. The coat is shaggy and grizzled brown or gray. The foreclaws are large, enabling the badger to excavate earth at incredible speed. The weight ranges from 8 to 25 pounds.

Badgers feed mostly on small rodents and rattlesnakes. They often occupy the burrows they create when digging out their prey. Ranchers dislike these animals because of the danger their burrows pose to hoofed livestock.

Man is the badgers' principal enemy, and they're still legally hunted and trapped in some places within their range, which includes most of the midwestern and western states and parts of the western Canadian provinces.

Some hunters find a great deal of pleasure in photographing wildlife, either in conjunction with hunting or as a separate activity. Almost every hunter has had reason to wish for a camera when an opportunity for an unusual photo presented itself. Taking camera equipment along adds a little weight, but considering what can result, it's worth the trouble. Shooting pictures from a blind seldom spooks game, and there are models made especially for the purpose.

12

FIREARMS SAFETY

There is no way to overemphasize firearms safety, because this is the single most important element related to the hunting and shooting experience. Guns are lethal weapons and must be regarded as such. Yet guns, like cars, aren't the cause of accidents. People are, and this is why it's vital that everyone operating and handling them be fully competent and aware of the safety rules. Even the best-trained and most responsible people have accidents. Among those who aren't, the incidence is vastly increased.

Ideally, firearms safety education should begin at home, because this is where more than 70 percent of the firearms deaths occur each year. People have guns for both personal protection and recreational purposes, and they are present in over 75 percent of the homes in the U.S. Because of this, some of the rules of safety practiced in the field must also be observed in the home. There are courses available for home firearms safety, and every state's wildlife agency can supply details on them.

The purpose is to educate people of all ages, with special emphasis on making children aware of the dangers posed by guns. Most youngsters, particularly boys, play with toy pistols or rifles, and unless otherwise instructed, they often make no distinction between play guns and real ones. Through a home safety course, lessons can be taught that will serve them well throughout their lives.

For example, it should be explained why it is important not to point guns at anyone. It's hard to enforce, since kids like to play games fashioned after what they see on television or in movies, much of which involves violence. It's worth the effort, though, and it can be effective if approached in a reasonable and diplomatic manner.

In the process of this, the dangers of real guns can be made clear, because it's quite possible they will be encountered sometime in one way or another. Responsible parents keep firearms safely locked away, but there are too many households where loaded guns are left in dresser drawers or other places of easy access. Curious or angry children can get hold of them, often with tragic consequences.

A hunter safety instructor supervises a young shooter on his first visit to the rifle range.

Unfortunately, both the media and the general public too frequently choose to place the blame on guns rather than human error or behavior. In so doing, they portray guns as bad, and those who teach or instruct youths must overcome this negative impression. The truth is that it is the proper handling and use of a gun that is the determining factor in a supportive value judgment.

Once the basics are covered, the best way to put children on the right track is to let them shoot at targets or plink with an air gun. That's the real "grabber" in conveying the positive aspects of guns and shooting, focusing on the fun and satisfaction of developing skills. And whether or not they eventually become avid hunters or shooters, they have been introduced to guns from a healthy perspective.

Early shooting training can be conducted in the home by using kits that provide everything necessary to help youngsters from 8 to 15 learn marksmanship and gun-handling techniques. This is a basic step that was introduced by Daisy Manufacturing Company more than 40 years ago as a part of the company's successful youth shooting-education program. This aggressive and successful endeavor has assisted in the training of millions of youngsters.

A young shooter tries his hand at shooting an air gun with a little help from an adult instructor.

Also, for more than 25 years, Daisy and the U.S. Jaycees have co-sponsored a program that begins with grass-roots shooting-education classes and ends with the International BB Gun Championships. It attracts participants from all over the world. The cooperation has extended to other groups, and it now enjoys the sponsorship of the Boy Scouts of America, 4-H, National Rifle Association, National Guard, American Legion, and many other schools, camps, clubs, and civic groups. There's plenty of opportunity available for kids to learn shooting and gun handling.

However, once youngsters have been schooled in the basics, the next step should be enrollment in the Hunter Education Program that is offered in every state. In almost all of them, it is mandatory that all young and new hunters possess a certificate of completion before being allowed to purchase a hunting license. As time passes, the percentage of hunters in the field who have received firearms training will steadily increase.

The first state-sponsored hunter safety program was offered in 1945, and the initial mandatory program began in 1949. Since 1978, hunter safety courses have been available in all 50 states, and more than 16 million youths have received instruction. Presently over 700,000 students get certificates each year.

Just as impressive, the Hunter Education Association reports that by 1988 the number of hunting-related fatalities had declined by 50 percent during a 30-year period. Much of this can be directly attributed to the hunter safety courses, since juveniles under the age of 21 cause about 40 percent of the hunting accidents, and this is the age group directly targeted by the program.

While hunter education is aimed primarily at youths, many adults take the course, sometimes along with their sons and daughters. In some cases it's a refresher, but just as often it's the parent's initial exposure to information on firearms handling and use.

Although the fundamentals of gun handling, cleaning, shooting and marksmanship are vital, the course includes much more. Students are taught what responsibilities they have to themselves and others, to property owners, and to the land itself. The basics of game management and wildlife identification are covered, as well as various problems a hunter may encounter in the field that require special attention, such as hypothermia or snakebite. There are also tips on hunting, as well as field-dressing game and care of meat.

The full gamut of hunting weapons is covered: modern rifles, shotguns and handguns; muzzleloaders; bow-hunting equipment; and the various kinds of ammunition and projectiles they utilize. There is even information on the safe operation of off-road vehicles, all-terrain vehicles and boats which hunters use as means of transportation.

There are many other safety courses offered throughout the country, sponsored or sanctioned by reputable organizations, and all have value. Some are designed principally to instruct people on gun use for self or home protection, and these are also valuable. Anything that promotes more responsible and safe handling and care of firearms is welcome.

Many versions of The Ten Commandments of Firearms Safety exist, but all have essentially the same message. One of the most simply stated and understandable of these is the one produced by the National Shooting Sports Foundation:

1. Always keep the muzzle pointed in a safe direction.
   This is the most basic gun safety rule. If everyone handled his firearm so carefully that the muzzle never pointed at something he didn't intend to shoot, there would be virtually no firearms accidents. It's as simple as that, and it's up to you. A safe direction means a direction in which a bullet cannot possibly strike anyone, taking into account possible ricochets, and the fact that bullets can penetrate walls and ceilings. Make it a habit to know exactly where the muzzle of your gun is pointing at all times, and be sure that you are in control of the direction in which the muzzle is pointing, even if you fall or stumble.

2. Firearms should be unloaded when not actually in use.
   Firearms should be loaded only when you are in the field or on a target range or shooting area, ready to shoot. Firearms and ammunition should be secured in a safe place, separate from each other, when not in use. Unload your gun immediately when you have finished shooting, well before you bring it into a car, camp or home. Whenever you handle a firearm, or hand it to someone, always open the action immediately, and visually check the chamber, receiver, and magazine to be certain they do not contain any ammunition. Never assume a gun is unloaded— check for yourself! Never push or pull a firearm toward yourself or another person.

Since Kolpin's gun boot can be padlocked, it's a safe way to store a firearm when not in use.

3. Don't rely on your gun's safety.

   Treat every gun as though it can fire at any time, regardless of the pressure on the trigger. The "safety" on a gun is a mechanical device that, like any such device, can become inoperable at the worst possible time. Besides, by mistake, the safety may be "off" when you think it's "on." The safety serves as a supplement to proper handling, but cannot possibly serve as a substitute for common sense. Never touch the trigger on a firearm until you actually intend to shoot. Keep fingers away from the trigger while loading or unloading.

4. Be sure of your target and what's beyond it.

   No one can call a shot back. Once a gun fires, you have given up all control over where the shot will go or what it will strike. Don't shoot unless you know exactly what your shot is going to strike. Be sure that your bullet will not injure anyone or anything beyond your target. No target or animal is so important that you do not have the time before you pull the trigger to be absolutely certain of your target and where your shot will stop.

5. Use correct ammunition.

   You must assume the serious responsibility of using only the correct ammunition for your firearm. Read and heed all warnings including those that appear in the gun's instruction manual and on the ammunition boxes. Improper or incorrect ammunition can destroy a gun and cause serious injury. Use only the ammunition that exactly matches the caliber or gauge or your gun.

6. If your gun fails to fire when the trigger is pulled, handle with care!
Occasionally, a cartridge may not fire when the trigger is pulled. If this
occurs, keep the muzzle pointed in a safe direction. Keep your face away
from the breech. Then carefully open the action, unload the firearm,

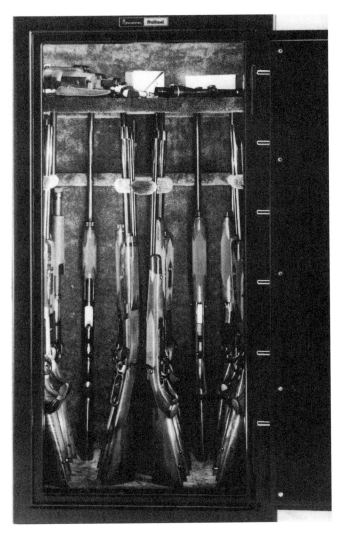

*One of the best ways to keep firearms safely stored is in a gun
vault.*

and dispose of the cartridge in a safe way. Any time there is a cartridge in the chamber, your gun is loaded and ready to fire—even if you've tried to shoot and it did not go off.

7. Always wear eye and ear protection when shooting.

All shooters should wear protective shooting glasses and some form of hearing protection while shooting. Exposure to shooting noise can damage hearing, and adequate vision protection is essential. Shooting glasses guard against twigs, falling shot, clay target chips, and the rare ruptured case or firearm malfunction.

8. Be sure the barrel is clear of obstructions before shooting.

Before you load your firearm, open the action and be certain that no ammunition is in the chamber or magazine. Then glance through the barrel to be sure it is clear of any obstruction. Even a small bit of mud, snow, excess lubricating oil, or grease in the bore can cause dangerously increased pressures, causing the barrel to bulge or even burst on firing, which can cause injury to the shooter and bystanders.

9. Don't alter or modify your gun, and have guns serviced regularly.

Firearms are complicated mechanisms that are designed by experts to function properly in their original condition. Any alterations or changes made to firearms after manufacture can make the gun dangerous and usually void of any factory warranties. Do not jeopardize your safety or the safety of others by altering the trigger, safety or other mechanism of any firearm or allowing unqualified persons to repair or modify them. Your gun is a mechanical device, which will not last forever, and is subject to wear. As such, it requires periodic inspection, adjustment, and service. Check with the manufacturer of your firearm for recommended servicing.

10. Learn the mechanical and handling characteristics of the firearm you are using. Not all firearms are the same. The method of carrying and handling firearms varies in accordance with the mechanical characteristics of each gun. Since guns can be so different, no person should handle any firearm without first having thoroughly familiarized himself with the particular type of firearm he is using, the safe-gun handling rules for loading, unloading, carrying, handling that firearm, and the rules of safe gun handling in general.

A couple of rules should be added:

Make absolutely certain that all guns and ammunition be kept under lock and key in the home. Some people take a loaded gun out at night for the reason of home protection, but if this is the case, it should be immediately locked up again in the morning.

It's vital for those shooters who reload, that extreme caution be exhibited in the loading process and that all components are boldly and accurately marked. For the safety of others, it's also very important that gunpowder, percussion caps and anything else that could endanger children or others be locked up so there is no access to them.

ETHICS

E thics refer to moral standards, which in turn relate directly to how a person behaves. Taken one step further, ethics are closely linked to responsibility.

Each individual has a set of personal ethics to use as a guide, but in almost all areas of human activity there are also stated ethics. These spell out the rules of behavior that apply in a given situation.

Hunting is one of these, and while some of the rules of the sport simply suggest things that one should remember to do or not to do, others are matters of law. Because of this, sometimes violation of the rules is more than unethical—it's illegal!

The things that require personal judgment are contained in what is basically an unwritten hunter's code. This relates to performing in a manner that is both fair and safe, and it includes not only the individual hunter and others, but also the game being sought. It's sort of an extension of the Golden Rule: a matter of conscience.

When it comes to those rules that must be followed, there is occasionally a conflict between what some regard as rights as opposed to privileges. Rights are those things provided citizens by the Constitution or other laws, and in the case of hunting, the most prominent example is ownership of land. One cannot trespass on private land without the permission of the owner, and it is that person's right to make the decision. Granting it is a privilege extended to the hunter. Briefly stated, rights cannot be taken away or violated; privileges are benefits either extended or earned.

One of a hunter's first responsibilities is to be thoroughly familiar with the laws governing seasons, bag limits, legal hours, trespass laws, license requirements and any special regulations. Going afield without this knowledge will inevitably lead to violations, and the buck definitely stops with the guilty individual. A good hunter is a well-informed hunter.

Something else that must be remembered: Hunters are under much more scrutiny by the general public than before, and examples of unethical or illegal activities generate heated criticism by various anti-hunting organizations. While the majority of Americans still favor hunting, the edge over those who consider it wrong isn't substantial. There are various reasons for their opposition, some of which are focused on killing animals, and others that are mainly anti-gun arguments. Yet there is strong objection to the irresponsible acts of hunters. It's plain to see that those who commit these violations of either ethics or laws are enemies of the millions of responsible people who cherish the sport.

What many nonhunters fail to understand is that killing animals isn't the sole purpose of hunting. Many people prefer to eat wild game they collect rather than meat harvested commercially. To them, it is tastier, and nutritionists have proved that it's healthier. Others consider game a special treat on the table.

That's just one facet of the picture, and not always the most important. Just getting out and enjoying the outdoors is a great and satisfying pleasure. For example, the thrill of an October day with clear, blue skies, blazing leaf color and the scent of autumn is a matchless experience. For some, it also offers the opportunity to test their stalking, tracking or calling skills. Others like to view and photograph wildlife. And being afield with friends affords a kind of comradeship not found elsewhere.

Hunting is a heritage that's precious to those who participate, but like anything of great value, it must be protected. To accomplish this, each individual must recognize those areas to which must be paid particular attention.

PERSONAL RESPONSIBILITY

Each hunter is liable for his own actions in the field, and it is important that attention be paid to making each outing as safe and successful as possible. Small-game and varmint hunters sometimes aren't subject to some of the laws that apply to big-game hunters, particularly in regard to wearing blaze orange or some other brightly colored cap or garment. However, rabbit hunters are advised to do so, since heavy cover can make it difficult to see companions, or for them to see you.

If going afield alone, it's wise to advise someone of where you will be hunting. That way if some accident should occur, whether it is a physical injury or an automobile problem, you can be located. This precaution can be a lifesaver, but in any case, it can save a lot of worry on the part of family or friends.

Cell phones or radios can be useful in some situations, and when two or more hunters are in the field together, the use of small, compact walkie-talkie units assures contact when separated.

Finally, as mentioned in previous chapters, a fanny pack or small day pack containing a first-aid kit, flashlight, and emergency blanket can be an invaluable addition to your standard gear.

RESPONSIBILITY TO LANDOWNERS

Small game and varmint hunters use private lands to a greater extent than big game hunters, so this source of access is of great importance. The only way it can be maintained and perpetuated is by not only respecting the rights of the landowners, but also making an effort to establish a good personal relationship with them.

First of all, most states require hunters to have written permission before entering private land, and ordinarily signs posting the property state this. However, even if there are no posted signs, the law still applies. In other words, just because you don't see a "No Hunting" doesn't mean you can trespass.

Responsible hunters always ask permission before hunting on private land. Because varmint hunters do landowners a favor, they sometimes get access to lands otherwise posted to all hunting.

Violations of this law by the few who do it lead to consequences that affect all hunters. Much of the private land on which no hunting is allowed became forbidden ground because of hunter abuses. No one can blame landowners for taking such action, and in most cases there is no way to undo the damage.

When granted the privilege of hunting on private land, the individual must conduct himself properly and respect any conditions the landowner may

The author talks with a farmer about getting rid of some woodchucks that have invaded his soybean fields.

state in regard to the use of his property. The hunter should take care not to damage fences, leave gates open, shoot in the direction of farm buildings or livestock, damage crops, leave any sort of litter (including spent rifle or shotgun shells), or violate any of the game laws. Too, rabbit or squirrel hunters should offer to share some of the game with their host. It helps cement a relationship and opens the door for future hunts.

Many hunters make visits to private property owners well ahead of the season in order to get acquainted and request permission. This gives the landowner the opportunity to size up the individual and decide if he wants him as a guest. Sometimes this pays off very well, because for safety's sake, many landowners restrict hunting privileges to only a small number of people.

RESPONSIBILITY TO PUBLIC LANDS

Some of the lands most valuable to hunters are the state and federal forests, parks and refuges, since these belong to the public and are accessible to everyone. They are places a hunter can depend upon when no other options can be found. And often, the potential in such places is as good as can be found anywhere.

However, such lands serve many purposes, only one of which is hunting; so while they're available to hunters, they're not their exclusive domain. They also provide a variety of other recreational opportunities—fishing, camping, hiking, nature and wildlife photography—as well as being water sources for domestic and agricultural uses, lumbering and grazing lands.

One of the most common problems on these public lands is vandalism, and hunters often get the blame for some of the things that occur. Shooting signs is one, since it's easy to link this with hunters, even though other people may be responsible. Campground littering is rampant, as well as the accidental or deliberate setting of wildfires. The only thing hunters can do to offset bad impressions is to go the extra mile and set the best possible examples of proper behavior and respect for these invaluable public lands. Without them, everyone who loves the outdoors would suffer.

RESPONSIBILITY TO WILDLIFE

Whether the animal or bird being sought is game or varmint, it is the hunter's obligation to try to harvest it as cleanly and humanely as possible. This means that skill in shooting should be attained before going into the field, because inaccurate shots are what cause unnecessary crippling. Injured animals or birds often escape, only to die slowly or suffer for long periods. Sometimes this can't be prevented, but being proficient in the use of guns is important.

When crippling occurs, one of the other talents every good hunter should possess comes into play. Competence in tracking can make it possible to retrieve game that otherwise would be lost.

To achieve full competence in the field, it's essential to be very well informed about the creature being hunted. Having this knowledge contributes to the success rate and enhances personal satisfaction. Hunting is a battle of wits, and if one doesn't understand the habits and behavior of the animal or bird he's seeking, there's a good chance of coming up empty-handed.

Taking home game for the family to enjoy is a bonus, yet just how flavorful it will be depends upon how it had been handled from the time of the kill until it arrives back home. Care of game will be discussed in another chapter,

Many state game agencies provide education classes on wildlife management.

but the point here is to recognize that mishandling game can make it unfit for consumption. Game should be seen as a prized possession and treated as such.

RESPONSIBILITY TO OTHER HUNTERS

Hunters can't always depend upon enjoying complete solitude, so the courtesy and respect extended to others who may be encountered in the field must be addressed.

First, you must remember that unless you happen to be the landowner, you're likely sharing the hunting area. It's preferable that it be seen this way, since then the two individuals or parties can meet and discuss the best way to divvy up the territory. Trying to compete generally leads to spoiling the hunt for all involved and can end up in arguments and even fights.

Many times these meetings result in friendships being created, some of which evolve into new hunting partnerships. Hunters are usually gregarious individuals, and when together there's ordinarily a high degree of compatibility. Visit any hunting camp and this will become apparent almost instantly.

The main thing is to have a positive attitude toward others in the field and to look out for their safety as well as yours. A hunter should not intrude on other hunters' territory or disturb game in that vicinity. Cooperation with others in the field begins when someone extends a friendly or helping hand. A responsible hunter will not hesitate to initiate this process.

IRRESPONSIBLE ACTIVITIES

There are many acts performed by hunters that constitute violations of either common sense or game laws. The disregard for safety rules is one of these, which can mean handling guns improperly; shooting without concern for what's in the background; firing randomly at whatever targets happen to appear, whether it be road signs or animals and birds that aren't the object of the hunt; and carrying loaded guns in the vehicle. Actually shooting from a vehicle or from a highway are illegal acts.

Some people pay no attention to seasons or bag limits, and these individuals are guilty of stealing game from honest hunters. They should be recognized as thieves, and a conscientious hunter will report them to authorities so they can be treated accordingly. In many cases, the game supply in any given area may not be able to be properly maintained if there is consistent poaching and over-limit kills.

Those individuals who commit irresponsible or illegal acts reflect badly on the hunting community and open the door for criticism from anti-hunting organizations. They prefer to portray all hunters as greedy, lawless slobs, so responsible hunters have a duty to reduce such incidents at every opportunity and educate others in the right way to do things.

RESPONSIBILITY TO HUNTING LAWS

Hunting laws are established for the benefit of both the hunter and wildlife species. Without such regulations, each would suffer, and it would be realistic to assume that the sport of hunting could disappear forever.

There is a good basis for such a prediction. In the past, over-hunting and lack of seasons and bag limits reduced some game birds and animals to near extinction, many of which have never recovered to the point where hunting them is feasible. It's obvious that some never will.

Game once flourished throughout North America, and there seemed to be an unending abundance. That was before the westward movement resulted in mass habitat destruction, which along with unregulated sport and market hunting seriously diminished the numbers of many of the species. The downward plunge continued until game laws were passed and management practices put into action. This came just in time for some species, but too late for others.

Today, the supply of game available to hunters is proof that these laws and regulations have been successful. The populations of many wildlife species are now larger than ever before, and areas where certain animals had been decimated have healthy numbers again as a result of restocking programs.

These things would not have been possible without hunter cooperation and the dollars they spend for licenses. That's why respect for the laws and good ethics is vital.

14

PROCESSING GAME

In earlier days when most of the population was rural, wild meat was a very important part of the diet. It was abundant and with no restrictions, so game could be gathered at any time. Later when hunting seasons were established, it remained on the menu throughout the year. Farm women canned, pickled, dried or smoked whatever species were found in the locations where they lived.

Usually, the happy chore of collecting squirrels and rabbits was assigned to the young boys. Before school, after school and on weekends, these youths could be found afield with their single-shot .22 rifles or shotguns. Farm families were typically large, so this meant a concerted effort to gather as much game as possible. Few boys backed off from the challenge. It beat baling hay and cleaning out barns by a mile!

Today, most hunters view the game they bag as a real bonus, and a special treat to be anticipated on the table. It can be a delicious and different addition to the regular meat fare, but only if it is properly handled and processed.

Otherwise it will end up being undesirable, if not unsuitable for consumption. Considering how negligent some hunters are in this department, it's no wonder that many people complain of the "wild taste" of game they are served.

Processing game correctly is one of the skills every hunter should perfect; it is equally as important as some of the others necessary for success. A conscientious hunter doesn't waste game, and allowing it to become tainted as a result of mishandling is much the same as throwing it away. That's what is going to happen eventually, anyway.

One of the main things to remember is that the more quickly the meat is cooled, the better the flavor will be. Some places have squirrel seasons that begin early in the fall, when temperatures are still very warm, and animals killed at these times should be gutted as soon as possible. Opening them up allows the heat to dispel much more rapidly. If this isn't done, the combination of body heat and air temperature will cause spoilage to begin within a very short time.

Even when cooler conditions exist, field dressing is still suggested. Often bullets or shot have penetrated intestines and allowed fluids to seep into the abdominal cavity. This can quickly contaminate the meat, so getting rid of this possibility quickly is well worthwhile.

For field-dressing small game, a big hunting knife is a disadvantage. A large blade isn't needed. The most useful knife is a small fixed-blade or folding model. Later, if the animal is to be skinned, a different choice of tools may be needed.

There's one exception to this. Rabbits can be field-dressed without a knife by using a unique method of removing the intestines. The way it's done is to grasp the animal just behind the front legs with one hand and squeeze hard. Then the left hand is placed below the right and also used to compress the insides toward the rear of the rabbit, making it protrude to more than twice its normal circumference.

While maintaining a tight squeeze hold, raise the rabbit overhead and swing down hard like driving with a golf club. The pressure causes the lower abdomen wall to tear, allowing the heart, lungs, liver and intestines to be thrown out. This takes care of the field dressing and lightens the load, since several rabbits can get heavy in a hurry! Incidentally, the heart and liver are very good to eat, so these items should be retained.

There are many knives and accessories that are useful in processing small game.

It isn't wise to place animals in plastic bags, since this will hold in body heat. Squirrel hunters often carry game on their belt, which permits plenty of airflow and more rapid cooling. Rabbit hunters can sometimes drop by their vehicle occasionally and put their game in the back of a truck or other open area.

Other than a knife and a small sharpener, it's convenient to carry along a few paper towels. These can be used to wipe the body cavity dry after field dressing, and can be buried afterward. Another handy item is the little pack-aged, pre-moistened towels for cleaning up the hands.

In order to keep the meat as clean as possible, it's better to wait until you're back home or in camp to skin animals. Leaving the hide on after field dressing doesn't hurt anything. Instead, it serves as a very suitable "wrapping." There are two schools of thought on the final job of skinning. Some hunters prefer to hang animals for a few days in a cool place before skinning; others like to complete this job as soon as possible. One thing to remember is that most small game animals have layers or pockets of excess fat. Take care to remove all of this, since it can adversely affect the flavor of the meat.

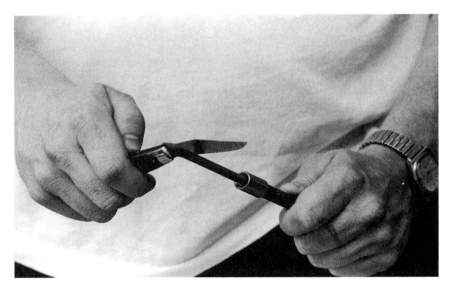

This diamond sharpener is only 4 inches long before assembled, and can be carried in a leather belt pouch.

Following are what most hunters think of as the best ways to finish the business of preparing game for consumption.

SQUIRRELS

Skinning squirrels is an easy matter if one of the two quickest methods is employed, since either of these can have the job done in minutes.

The first requires only that a slit be made in the skin across the lower back that's wide enough to admit a couple of fingers of both hands. With the fingers hooked in each side of the opening, pull in opposite directions and the hide can be peeled off in seconds.

Once this is done, the head, feet and tail can be cut off. After that, the body can be cut into pieces, rinsed off in cold water and placed in the refrigerator or prepared for cooking. Some hunters are fond of squirrel brains, and in this event, the head should also be skinned, cut off and added to the other edible parts.

The second approach is nearly as easy. Make a slit across the lower abdomen even with the anal opening, and then cut through the tail, being careful

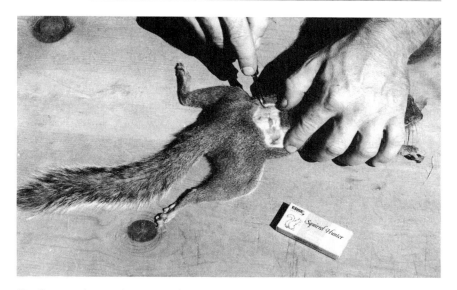

The first step is to make a 2– to three–inch slit across the back.

Next, pull in both directions, much like peeling off sweat pants and shirt.

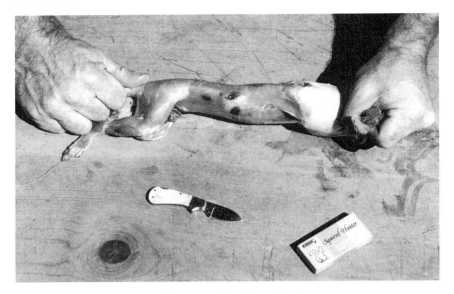

Skin out all but the last joint of the legs, the tail, and head.

Finally, cut off the legs, head, and tail, then remove the visceral material.

not to sever the skin on the opposite side. Once this is done, take hold of the back legs, place your foot on the tail, and pull. The skin will come off from the hindquarters forward. Skin out the front and back legs (and the head, if desired).

Both of these methods work best on freshly killed squirrels, because the skin comes off much more easily. The longer you wait, the harder the task becomes.

RABBITS

The skin of rabbits isn't as tough as that of a squirrel, so it isn't as easily removed. However, the technique of making a slit across the back and pulling in opposite directions will work okay. The problem is that the skin sometimes tears, but if the animal is warm, it's no trouble to get it all off fairly quickly.

Skinning rabbits almost always results in a lot of hair clinging to the membrane that surrounds the flesh. This can be removed with a stiff brush while it's being rinsed. If this doesn't work satisfactorily, a cloth dipped in scalding water will wipe away bits of fur that remain. This is a good procedure to use with any small game animal.

Rabbits sometimes carry tularemia, so as a precaution against infection, it's wise to use rubber gloves while cleaning them. If this isn't done, be sure to wash your hands thoroughly with strong soap after the procedure is completed.

Many people believe that letting rabbits remain in the refrigerator for several days before cooking causes the meat to be tenderer. The best way to store it is in water with a little salt added.

RACCOONS AND OPOSSUMS

Throughout the ranges of both of these species there are plenty of people who consider both to be excellent table fare. Raccoons in particular have been popular, and there are places where the meat has been commercially marketed. The biggest source of supply was trappers, who got a double benefit from the animals by being able to sell both the fur and the carcass.

There's no quick and easy way to skin raccoons, so whether it's the meat or the hide that's important, the procedure is much the same. Essentially, this requires making a cut from the vent up the back of both hind legs to the last joint. Another cut is made from the anal vent to the base of the neck. A cut halfway around the tail will allow the center portion to be pulled out. Then simply work off the hide and pull it over the head to the nose, cutting off the feet in the process.

Under the front armpits (or legpits), and on either side of the spine are small "kernels" or scent glands that should be excised.

Much the same technique can be used on opossums, except that there are no scent glands to be concerned with, and even if the hide is to be retained, it's not necessary to save the tail.

When the animal is skinned and rinsed off, remove the fat and cut it into pieces unless it is to be baked whole. A few days' refrigeration will probably help improve the quality. Unless the animals are obviously young, it's also wise to parboil the meat before final preparation. Old raccoons and opossums are very tough unless tenderized.

WOODCHUCKS

Woodchucks, especially young ones, are very fine eating, but getting the skin off the varmints is a tough chore! It has been said that the best way to accomplish it is "any way you can," but employing the same basic techniques used with raccoons will do. The difficulty is that the hide and flesh seem almost welded together.

Experienced hunters make an effort to take care of their woodchuck needs by concentrating on picking off young animals in spring and early summer. That way the problem of having to parboil the meat is averted.

Once it is skinned, the scent glands should be removed and the animal cut up and soaked in a mild saline solution for a couple of days.

BEAVER

The meat of beaver is a sort of "sleeper," since few hunters think of it as table fare. However, the meat is rich and very flavorful, and making an effort to harvest a couple of young animals can result in a culinary treat.

The standard skinning routine used on all but squirrels and rabbits should be used, and since some people regard the tail as gourmet fare, it can also be skinned out. There are castor glands at the base of the tail that should be removed, and while young animals seldom have much excess fat, get rid of any that's present.

For most recipes, the animal should be cut into portions, but many cooks prefer whole roasted beavers. In either case, soaking for at least 24 hours in salt water with about 1/4 cup of vinegar will be beneficial.

MUSKRAT

Many older hunters have had plenty of experience skinning muskrats, since at one time trapping these animals was the main source of spending money for farm youths. Probably a lot of them also had the pleasure of eating muskrats, the meat of which is similar in texture and taste to that of squirrels, except a bit darker.

For the uninitiated, skinning is an easy process, especially if you aren't trying to keep the hide, and the method of slitting the skin across the back and stripping off the hide is as good as any.

Take care to remove the scent glands, which are much like those on raccoons, except there are also some on the lower part of the belly. Once these are out of the way, cut the meat into pieces, which generally amounts to six: the four legs, loin and rib cage. Then soak in a mild salt and vinegar solution that helps tenderize the meat and draw out any remaining blood from the meat.

SELECTED RECIPES

Cooking and eating game doubles the pleasure of the hunt and provides enjoyment for those who get to share in the bounty. Wild game is much more nutritious than domestic meat, since it is free of chemical and organic additives. There are countless ways to cook wild game and enough different recipes to fill several books. However, picking out some that are traditional favorites will give a sampling of the culinary delights that can be created. Sitting down at the table to a dinner of savory game and all the trimmings is the best way to put the final cap on a hunting experience.

Here are some good ones to try:

SOUTHERN SQUIRREL 'N DUMPLINGS

2 squirrels, cut in serving pieces	8 carrots, split and halved
2 bay leaves	1 teaspoon salt
1 cup onions, sliced	1/2 teaspoon pepper
1 cup chopped celery	

Dumplings:

2 cups flour	4 teaspoon baking powder
1/2 teaspoon salt	3/4 cup milk

Cover squirrels with 1 inch water, add bay leaves and simmer for 1 1/4 hours. Skim fat, and then add onions, celery, carrots, salt and pepper. Add 1 1/2 cups water and cook for 15 minutes. To prepare dumplings, sift dry ingredients, and then add milk gradually. Roll on floured board until 1/2 inch thick. Cut into 3 inch squares and add to kettle contents. Cover and cook 15 minutes. Serves 4.

BATTER-FRIED SQUIRREL

2 squirrels, cut in serving pieces	1 carrot, sliced
4 cups boiling water	1 stalk celery, diced
1 onion, chopped	1 sprig fresh parsley, chopped

Batter:

1/2 cup flour	1/4 teaspoon salt
1/2 cup cornmeal	1 egg, lightly beaten
1 teaspoon baking powder	3/4 cup milk

Drop squirrel pieces into boiling water, add onion, carrot, celery, and parsley. Simmer until squirrel is tender. Pour off liquid and reserve for gravy. Refrigerate meat until cool. While meat is cooling, prepare batter: mix dry ingredients, combine milk with beaten egg, and then add to the flour mixture. Dry the meat, then dip in batter and deep-fry until nicely browned. Serve with your favorite cream-style gravy. Serves 4.

SQUIRREL STEW DIABLO

3 squirrels	1/4 cup diced celery
2 onions, chopped	4 tablespoon chili powder
1 green pepper, chopped	Salt and pepper to taste
1 jalapeno pepper, chopped	Dash Louisiana Hot Sauce
3 medium potatoes, diced	1 1/2 cups cooked rice

Cook squirrels in water to cover and cook until tender. Remove from water and refrigerate to cool, reserving broth. Remove meat from the bones and add to broth. Add onions, peppers, potatoes, celery and spices. Cook for 45 minutes. Serve hot over cooked rice. Serves 6.

BARBECUED RABBIT

3 pounds rabbit cut in serving pieces
Flour, salt and pepper   1/4 cup cooking oil
Your favorite barbecue sauce

Preheat oven to 325 degrees. Coat rabbit pieces in mixture of flour, salt and pepper. Heat oil in an oven-ready skillet. Add rabbit and brown on all sides over moderate heat. Pour barbecue sauce into pan and cover. Bake for 45 minutes, then uncover and brown under broiler for 10–15 minutes. Serves 6.

BRAISED RABBIT

5-pound rabbit split	2 sprigs fresh thyme
Salt and pepper to taste	1 carrot, diced
2 tablespoons vegetable oil	1/2 onion, chopped
1 cup consommé	

Preheat oven to 400 degrees. Heat oil in a heavy skillet. Add rabbit, sprinkle with salt and pepper, and brown on all sides. Meanwhile heat consommé with thyme for 5 minutes. Strain, then reheat and add carrot and onion. Put rabbit pieces into baking pan. Pour consommé mixture over rabbit. Cover and bake for 45 minutes, basting occasionally. Serves 4–6.

STEWED RABBIT IN JUICE

2 rabbits cut in serving pieces	1/2 cup water
1/4 cup vegetable oil	1/2 cup pear juice
2 large onions, diced	1/2 cup pineapple juice
2 cloves minced garlic	1 teaspoon salt
1/2 cup celery, diced	1/2 teaspoon pepper
8 ounce mushrooms, sliced	1/4 teaspoon thyme
2 tablespoons flour	

Brown rabbit in vegetable oil in a large skillet or Dutch oven. Remove meat. Sauté onions, garlic, celery, and mushrooms until tender. Add flour. Combine water, pear and pineapple juice and add gradually. Season with salt, pepper and thyme. Bring to a boil and simmer for five minutes. Add rabbit meat, cover, and simmer for 30–40 minutes until tender. Serves 4–6.

RACCOON AND SWEET POTATOES

1 raccoon	1 cup celery, diced
Vinegar	1 large onion, chopped
Water to cover	1 green pepper, chopped
Salt and pepper to taste	Vegetable oil
Cayenne pepper to taste	Flour
2 cloves minced garlic	4 medium sweet potatoes

Soak raccoon for one hour in a vinegar/water solution. Drain. Cut into serving pieces and place in a pan with water to cover. Add salt, pepper, cayenne, garlic, celery, onion, and green pepper. Boil until partially tender. Remove meat. Heat a small amount of vegetable oil in a skillet. Add raccoon and brown on all sides. Remove. Make thin gravy with flour and drippings. Place meat in roasting pan; add gravy. Bake at 350 degrees for 30 minutes. Peel and halve sweet potatoes. Place around meat in roasting pan. Continue baking until potatoes are done. Serves 4.

ROAST RACCOON 'N DRESSING

1 raccoon
Water to cover
Vinegar

1 teaspoon baking soda
Salt and pepper

Dressing:
3 cups dry bread crumbs
2 tablespoons melted butter
1 small onion, chopped

1 cooking apple, thinly sliced
1/2 teaspoon salt
1/4 teaspoon pepper

Preheat oven to 375 degrees. Parboil raccoon for 30 minutes in water and baking soda. Meanwhile, prepare dressing: combine bread crumbs, butter, onion, apple, salt and pepper; add water until moist. Drain meat. Rub inside and out with salt and pepper. Stuff with dressing; place in roasting pan and bake for 1 1/2 hours or until tender and nicely browned, skimming fat as it accumulates and adding water. Before serving, rub meat with a cloth soaked in vinegar. Serves 4.

RACCOON, CURRY STYLE

2 young raccoons
Salted water to cover
1 medium onion, quartered
1/4 teaspoon Tabasco sauce
3 tablespoons butter
4 tablespoons curry powder
2 cups chicken stock
2 tomatoes, diced

3 medium onions, chopped fine
1 tablespoon paprika
1 bay leaf
1 stick cinnamon
1 teaspoon salt
1 lemon, thinly sliced
1 cup sour cream

Heat salted water, onion and Tabasco sauce. Add raccoon and parboil for 30 minutes. Cool meat, remove from bones, and cut in 1-inch cubes. Brown butter in large skillet; add curry powder and meat. Stir over heat until mixture is dark. Add stock, tomatoes, onions, seasonings and lemon. Simmer until meat is tender. Reduce heat; add sour cream. Remove when heated through, but not boiling. Serves 4–6.

ROAST STUFFED OPOSSUM

1 opossum
Salt and pepper

1 quart water

Dressing:
1 tablespoon vegetable oil
1 onion, chopped
Opossum liver
1 cup bread crumbs

1/4 teaspoon Worcestershire sauce
1 hard-boiled egg, chopped
1 teaspoon salt

Preheat oven to 350 degrees. Wash the cleaned opossum in soda water. Rub inside and out with salt and pepper. To prepare dressing, sauté onion in oil; add opossum liver and cook until tender; chop liver. Remove from heat. Mix together bread crumbs, Worcestershire sauce, egg, and salt, adding water to moisten. Add sautéed liver and onions. Stuff opossum with dressing; truss. Place on rack in roasting pan and add 1 quart water. Roast 2 1/2 hours or until tender, basting every 15 minutes. Serves 4–6.

GRANNY'S OPOSSUM AND YAMS

1 opossum
Salt and pepper to taste
Flour
1/2 cup water

4 medium yams
1/4 teaspoon salt
2 tablespoons brown sugar

Preheat oven to 350 degrees. Rub salt-pepper mixture over opossum inside and out. Coat inside and out with flour. Place the opossum on its back in a roasting pan; add water. Cover and bake for 45 minutes. Peel yams, split lengthwise, and place in pan around edge. Add water if needed. Continue baking for 30 minutes; remove cover. Sprinkle yams with salt and brown sugar. Bake uncovered until meat and yams are brown and tender. Serves 4.

APPLE-ROASTED OPOSSUM

1 young opossum
Stuffing (your recipe)
Bacon strips
3 cups water
1 tablespoon sugar

1 tablespoon lemon juice
6 apples, pared and quartered
1 cup brown sugar
1 teaspoon lemon rind
1 teaspoon ground cinnamon

Preheat oven to 350 degrees. Stuff cleaned opossum; place on rack in roaster and cover with bacon. Add sugar and lemon juice to water; pour into bottom of roaster. Bake for 2 hours. Drain all but 1 cup of liquid from pan. Surround opossum with apples. Mix together brown sugar, lemon rind and cinnamon; sprinkle on apples. Continue roasting for 30 minutes or until meat is tender. Serves 4.

WOODCHUCK ITALIANO

1 woodchuck	1 clove minced garlic
8 cups water	Salt and pepper to taste
1/2 cup salt	1/2 cup vinegar
4 mint leaves	2 cups tomato sauce
1/4 cup olive oil	1 teaspoon basil

Soak dressed chuck overnight in cold water and salt. Remove, cut in 8 pieces and boil 15 minutes in clear water. Rinse meat, return to salted water and repeat soaking process. Rinse again; boil in clear water with mint leaves for 45 minutes; drain. Salt and pepper both sides and brown in skillet with oil and garlic. Add vinegar; cover and simmer 8 minutes. Remove to cooking pot. Add tomato sauce and basil. Cook over moderate heat for 1 1/2 hours. Serves 4–6.

WOODCHUCK BURGERS

Ground meat of 1 woodchuck	1 tablespoon melted butter
1/2 cup fresh bread crumbs	White corn meal
1/2 cup onion, diced	3 tablespoon vegetable oil
1 teaspoon salt	1 cup catsup
1/4 teaspoon pepper	1/2 teaspoon Worcestershire sauce
2 eggs	

Preheat oven to 325 degrees. Beat one egg. Combine ground meat, bread crumbs, onion, salt, pepper, egg, and butter. Mix well and shape into 8 patties. Beat remaining egg. Dip patties into egg, then coat with corn meal. Fry until brown in hot oil. Mix catsup and Worcestershire sauce together and pour over patties. Bake for 1 hour. Serves 8.

WOODCHUCK IN SOUR CREAM SAUCE

1 woodchuck cut in serving pieces   6 peppercorns
Water to cover   6 whole allspice
1 small onion, sliced   1/4 cup vinegar
1 teaspoon salt   1 tablespoon flour
4 laurel leaves   1 1/2 cups sour cream

Put chuck pieces in deep pan; cover with water. Add onions, seasonings and vinegar. Simmer until meat is tender. Remove meat. strain stock and return to pan. Mix together flour and sour cream; add to simmering stock. Add meat; heat thoroughly, but do not allow to boil. Serves 4–6.

ROAST BEAVER

1 beaver   1/3 cup diced onion
Water to cover   1/3 cup diced carrot
1/4 cup vinegar   1/3 cup diced celery
Salt and pepper   Flour
1/4 pound salt pork cut in strips

Remove all surface fat from beaver; soak overnight in water mixed with vinegar. Preheat oven to 350 degrees. Remove meat, rinse, place on rack in roaster. Cut several slits in meat and rub with salt and pepper; cover slits with salt pork, and dust with a little flour. Add 1/2 cup water to pan; cover. Roast for 30 minutes. Add more water if needed. Sprinkle diced vegetables over meat. Continue roasting uncovered until meat falls off the bones. Use pan juices for gravy. Serves 4–6.

ONION-FRIED BEAVER

1 beaver   2 tablespoons butter
Salted water to cover   Vegetable oil
3 bay leaves   Flour
4 cloves   Salt and pepper to taste
2 onions, sliced

Soak dressed beaver overnight in salted water; cut into serving pieces. Add bay leaves and cloves to clear water and parboil meat for 30 minutes. Meanwhile, sauté onion slices in butter and 2 tablespoons vegetable oil until translucent. Remove onions to another container. Add salt and pepper to flour. Dry meat pieces and roll in seasoned flour mixture. Fry in butter and oil until meat is brown. Top with sautéed onions. Serves 6.

BEAVER TAIL HENRI

1 beaver tail	Flour
1 cup red wine	1 beaten egg
1 cup water	1 cup cracker crumbs
1 large onion, chopped	3 tablespoons melted butter
1/2 cup vinegar	1 lemon, thinly sliced
1 teaspoon salt	

Marinate beaver tail for 24 hours in mixture of red wine, water, and onion. Preheat oven to 350 degrees. Dry tail and scrape carefully. Add vinegar and salt to enough water to cover the meat. Parboil until nearly tender. Dry tail again; coat lightly with flour. Dip meat into beaten egg, then into cracker crumbs. Place on rack in roasting pan; drizzle butter over meat. Roast until tender and nicely browned. Garnish with lemon slices before serving. Serves 2.

FRIED MUSKRAT WITH MILK GRAVY

2 muskrats, quartered	Flour
Water to cover	White corn meal
Salt and pepper	Vegetable oil
2 eggs, beaten	3 tablespoons flour
1/2 cup milk	1 1/2 cups milk

Soak muskrat pieces for 1 hour in salted water. Rinse and pat dry; sprinkle with salt and pepper. Blend beaten eggs with 1/2 cup milk. Dip meat in flour, then in egg mixture, then in corn meal. Brown on all sides in hot oil, then lower heat and simmer 1 hour. Remove meat; pour off oil, returning 3 tablespoons of the oil to skillet. Add remaining flour and milk to make milk gravy; cook until thickened. Serves 2.

BARBECUED MUSKRAT

4 muskrats

2 quarts water

2 cups vinegar

1/4 cup salt

Vegetable oil

Barbecue Sauce:

1/2 cup butter

1 large onion, grated

1/2 cup water

1 tablespoon Worcestershire sauce

3 tablespoons lemon juice

1 teaspoon salt

1/2 teaspoon pepper

2 teaspoons paprika

1/2 teaspoon dry mustard

1 tablespoon brown sugar

2 tablespoons tomato paste

Soak muskrat in water, vinegar and salt for up to 24 hours. Preheat oven to 350 degrees. Meanwhile, prepare barbecue sauce: sauté onion in butter until it is translucent; add remaining ingredients and simmer for 10 minutes. Drain muskrat and pat dry; cut in serving pieces. Brown on all sides in hot oil. Place in baking dish and cover with barbecue sauce; bake for 1 hour, basting frequently with sauce. Serves 4.

Here's an interesting "kicker" to the preceding ways to prepare game and varmint species:

There's the standing joke about "eating crow," but it turns out that there's a recipe that may put a different slant on the saying. In other words, they really can be eaten, and enjoyed!

"EAT CROW" CASSEROLE

6 crows

Salted water to cover

2 cans mushroom soup

2 cups cooked rice

Soak birds overnight in salt water. Rinse; simmer in clear water until tender; drain. Preheat oven to 350 degrees. Remove meat from bones. Heat soup in saucepan. Add 1/2 of the meat. Spread 1/2 of the rice in a casserole dish; add remaining meat. Form a second layer with the remaining rice; pour soup and meat mixture over all. Cover dish and bake for 15 minutes. Serves 3–6.

INDEX